U.S. Leadership in
Asia and the Middle East

THE CREDIBILITY OF INSTITUTIONS, POLICIES AND LEADERSHIP
A Series funded by the Hewlett Foundation
Kenneth W. Thompson, *Series Editor*

U.S. Leadership in Asia and the Middle East

The Credibility of Institutions, Policies and Leadership
Volume 18

**Edited by
Kenneth W. Thompson**

University Press of America
Lanham • New York • London

Library of Congress Cataloging in Publication Data
Main entry under title:

U.S. leadership in Asia and the Middle East.

(The Credibility of institutions, policies and
leadership ; v. 18)
"Co-published by arrangement with the White Burkett
Miller Center of Public Affairs, University of Virginia"—
T.p. verso.
Bibliography: p.
1. United States—Foreign relations—1945-   —Ad-
dresses, essays, lectures. 2. United States—Foreign
relations—Asia—Addresses, essays, lectures. 3. Asia—
Foreign relations—United States—Addresses, essays,
lectures. 4. United States—Foreign relations—Near
East—Addresses, essays, lectures. 5. Near East—Foreign
relations—United States—Addresses, essays, lectures.
I. Thompson, Kenneth W., 1921-   . II. Title: US
leadership in Asia and the Middle East. III. Series.
E840.U174   1985   327.73056   85-670
ISBN 0-8191-4426-6 (alk. paper)
ISBN 0-8191-4427-4 (pbk. : alk. paper)

Table of Contents

v

Preface

A discussion of leadership and the United States which constitutes the subject matter of Part Four in the Hewlett Series must of necessity deal with American leadership in the world. Although some critics proclaim that the United States engages itself too broadly in world leadership playing the role of global policeman, that criticism is unlikely to lead to the disengagement of the United States. Nor can critics for an opposing view that the United States is entering an era of neo-isolationism and must undertake to resume effective world leadership force any administration to act as though it had unlimited power everywhere in the world. Somewhere between globalism and neo-isolationism most administrations are likely to take their stands. A discussion of American leadership from a functional standpoint—strategy and law—and as that leadership has manifested itself in two crucial world regions may further understanding of the possibilities and limits of U.S. leadership. To know where we have been from the standpoint of leadership may help us understand where we can lead in the future.

Introduction

The authors of the present volume approach world leadership from two broad perspectives. The first looks at leadership from a functional standpoint. The second examines U.S. leadership in two crucial regions of the world.

One aspect of functional leadership is strategic thinking. Another is the outlook of international law. An important expression of strategic thinking is NSC-68, a study prepared in the Truman administration which sought to give worldwide content to the containment doctrine. In order to affect leadership, a group was formed "to sell NSC-68." Nelson Drew who is a professor at the Airforce Academy in Colorado traces this process as it unfolded.

Another study examines the role that international law can and should play in providing a leadership role for the United States in the nuclear age. Bill Parson is a young international lawyer who holds a responsible position in the Center for Law and National Security at the University of Virginia Law School. Having reviewed the possible theories concerning the place of international law, Parsons offers an original viewpoint regarding what law can do in the shaping of nuclear policies.

Two outstanding young Chinese scholars from Taiwan help Americans understand two vital foreign policy choices the U.S. has made in Asia. The first case study presented by Mr. Lin looks in some depth at the 1958 Quemoy-Matsu crisis and U.S. leadership in coping with that conflict. His colleague, Mr. Kao, offers a second case study in a penetrating review of U.S. strategic policy toward occupied Japan.

Finally, Mr. Riley takes us back to the 1973 Middle Eastern War to examine the Soviet bid for leadership in an important crisis and the success of the United States and Israel in turning back the Russians. While other important developments have occured in the past several years, the analysis of a specific crisis helps readers to understand forces at work in the region and the importance for the United States to keep an upper hand.

PART ONE

Leadership in
Security Policy

The Selling of NSC-68: The Public Case for the Militarization of Containment

S. NELSON DREW

I. THE GOVERNMENT, THE MEDIA, AND PUBLIC OPINION

On the 31st of January, 1950, President Harry S. Truman called upon the Departments of State and Defense to "undertake a re-examination of our objectives in peace and war, and of the effects of these objectives on our strategic plans, in light of the probable fission bomb capability ... of the Soviet Union" (FRUS, 1950: Vol I, 142). Over the next two and one half months, a small group of men who constituted what was known as the "State-Defense Policy Review Group" labored in response to the President's directive. Their efforts resulted in a document which was described by Secretary of State Dean Acheson as "one of the most important documents in American history" (Nathan and Oliver, 1981: 116, note 72). The document was NSC-68.

The document itself, consisting of some 66 pages, was classi-fied "Top Secret." But it was never intended that its contents should be withheld from public knowledge. NSC-68 was, as John Lewis Gaddis put it, "as much a work of advocacy as of analysis" (1982: 106). It was, in many respects, a call to arms for the Ameri-can people, asking their support in what has been labeled "the militarization of containment" (Sanders, 1983: 23). The perception that such a public call was necessary is made explicit in the text of NSC-68 itself, in language which might well have been taken directly from a treatise on democracy written during the founding of our country:

> The full power which resides within the American people will be evoked only through the traditional demo-cratic process: this process requires, firstly, that sufficient

information regarding the basic political, economic, and military elements of the present situation be made publicly available so that an intelligent popular opinion may be formed. Having achieved a comprehension of the issues now confronting the Republic, it will then be possible for the American people and the American Government to arrive at a consensus. Out of this common view will develop a determination of the national will and a solid, resolute expression of that will. The initiative in this process lies with the government. (NSC-68, in FRUS: 1950, Vol I; p. 254)

It is the manner in which the government sought to exercise this "initiative" in developing a "consensus" on the "determination of the national will" which forms the central focus of this paper. In particular, I hope to show that NSC-68 represents a classic example of the process by which the government can exercise leadership of public opinion through the use of the mass media and opinion elites within the population itself. At the same time, it should become obvious that in exercising such leadership, the government is faced with some serious constraints, not the least of which are the effects of having "oversold" its previous policy positions.

The role played by the mass media and public opinion in the formation of American foreign policy is an elusive one. To be sure, there is no lack of expressed opinion on the issue. It is a rare government leader in this country who has not at some point in his or her career commented upon the importance (or lack thereof) of generating media and public support for crucial policy decisions. The same might well be said for leading members of the press. Yet careful studies of the exact nature of the relationship assumed by such comments are scarce. Moreover, the studies that do exist do not necessarily agree among themselves.

Some studies of the relationship refer to the media as conduits of information, providing the basis upon which informed public opinion can be generated and then translated into action by a responsive government (Cohen, 1963: 22-25). Others see the media as a power unto themselves, creating public opinion and setting an agenda which both constrains and demands government action (Graber, 1980: 132-134). Yet a third view describes the media as part of the "establishment," working with or used by the government to create public opinion which supports policies already determined within closed government circles (Paletz and Entman, 1981: "Part Two: The Media Manipulators", 29–124).

The point of view which is by far the most widely expressed among those working within the media is that which depicts the media as relatively neutral channels of information to the public. This is the view which Bernard Cohen describes as "the classic justification in American democratic thought for a free press" (1963: 5). The central thrust of its thesis is that for the democratic process to work, the government must be able to follow the lead of informed public opinion in developing policy, and that such opinion will provide the support necessary to execute that policy. A television documentary on "The Press and the People," produced in the late 1950s by WGBH, Boston, captured the essence of this argument in its introduction:

> Today and every day, the American people must make decisions on which their whole survival may depend. To make sound decisions the people must be informed. For this, they depend on the nation's free press (quoted in Cohen, 1963: 5).

The media are not the only ones who provide support for this interpretation of the role of public opinion in the foreign policy process. In August of 1949, for example, President Harry Truman opened a news conference with the remarks that:

> My primary purpose ... is to ensure that our policy shall be based on informed and intelligent public opinion. This is the way in which our system of government acquires its strength. ... In this nation, foreign policy is not made by the decisions of a few. It is the result of the democratic process, and represents the collective judgement of the people (Public Papers, 1949: 408–409).

Although the logic which supports this concept may appear to be sound, there are some serious problems with this "classic justification" as a model to explain the relationships among the government, media, and public in the development of American foreign policy. To begin with, on most matters of foreign policy there is evidence that the bulk of the American public is neither informed nor interested. As one recent study observes, "in no area of public policy are most Americans so ill-informed and unconcerned as in foreign policy" (Nathan and Oliver, 1983: 249). This certainly seems to be the view of news editors in this country, who, according to Doris Graber, "routinely judge audience interest in foreign news to be below interest in local and national news, sports, and comics" (1980: 244). The opinions of these editors are critical, because they act upon their views to decide what news to print and broadcast. On an average, only 11% of all stories in American newspapers and 16% of all nightly newscast items are devoted to foreign affairs (Graber, 1980: 244).

Such a level of interest and available information hardly seems compatible with the needs of a people who must daily "make decisions on which their whole survival may depend." In fact, as most studies of foreign policy decision-making indicate, "the American people" as a whole are rarely, if ever, directly involved in making such decisions. Those decisions are made by their elected and appointed representatives in Washington, who may or may not be considering public opinion at the time they are making them.

This is not to say that such decision-makers are unconcerned with public opinion. However, the views they are most likely to be aware of are those which exist among what have come to be called "opinion elites," consisting of the relatively small segment of the population who make a point both of following foreign policy issues as they develop and of making their opinions on those issues known.[1] In some cases, the members of this "opinion elite" may include prominent columnists and broadcast journalists from within the media establishment itself. In other instances, citizens groups and lobbyists may constitute the core of "informed public opinion" on an issue. Only rarely, however, will the mass public on its own initiative seize upon an issue as a result of information in the press and create the sort of pressure which demands a response from the government.

While those within the news industry may be most prone to describe their roles in terms of creating an informed public, the model which is most often reflected in the statements of those charged with making foreign policy decisions tends to resemble more closely the "agenda-setting" view of the media. They see the press as setting an agenda for public discussion and government action through the use of its influence to establish which issues and

values are important at any given point in time. The media are said
to enjoy this power by virtue of their ability to determine what is
and what is not "news." The core of this point of view is reflected
in the belief that, as Bernard Cohen puts it:

> Generally . . . the world of foreign policy reaches us—
> or those of us who are interested and attentive—via
> the media of mass communication. . . . And if we do not
> see a story in the newspapers (or catch it on radio or
> television), it effectively has not happened so far as we
> are concerned (1963: 13).

The crucial implication of this model, as far as government
policy-makers are concerned, is that the agenda thus set by the
media may or may not be conducive to the policies the government is attempting to pursue. In recent years, in fact, the dominant
view among many government officials has been that the media
agenda is more often than not openly hostile to the priorities of the
administration. Especially in those cases in which those in the
government perceive that their policy will require some level of
public support to succeed (i.e. through payment of increased taxes
or serving in the armed forces), part of the governmental program
may therefore include attempts to make the government's agenda
and the media agenda coincide. Frequently, such attempts become
a critical element in the plans of the executive branch to obtain
congressional approval for a new policy. In such cases, when it
may become necessary to convince congressmen that voting for
the administration's proposal will not cost them votes back home
(or, if possible, to show that failure to support the policy *will* cost
them votes), it is always useful to be able to demonstrate that the
concerns of the administration's agenda are the same as those of
the public and media agendas.

The degree to which the government is successful in getting its
agenda adopted by the media forms the foundation for the view
that the media, and through them public opinion, may be manipulated by an administration. While this view is seldom articulated by
those in either the media or government circles, it is a frequently
cited concern of both scholars and "concerned citizens" (Cohen,
1963: 28-30; Graber, 1980: 80-82; Paletz and Entman, 1981: 56-63).
Moreover, there are crucial elements in both the "informed public"
and the "agenda setting" models which contribute directly to creat-

ing conditions under which government efforts to influence the media agenda become possible.

To the extent that the media feels an obligation to serve as an information channel to the public, what the government is planning to do is news, and those who are charged with making foreign policy decisions are therefore news sources. Most of the foreign policy news published or broadcast in the United States actually originates in Washington (Graber, 1980: 254). As a result, a symbiotic relationship exists between foreign affairs correspondents and foreign policy-makers in the Washington community. Those in the government need the media to place their agenda items before the public and opinion elites. The reporters need the information their sources can supply. The result may appear to be collusion between the government and the media to manipulate public opinion, but it often is merely the outcome of a competitive news gathering process. As one candid news columnist observed, "if you have a policy, you have something to sell that makes a good story for a reporter" (Cohen, 1963: 29).

Neither side in this relationship is above using the other in the pursuit of its own goals. The media have their leaks and "unnamed sources" within the government which allow them to cover "news" that is in opposition to the officially promoted government policy. As Bernard Cohen observes, one of the features inherent in the American concept of a free press is that "here the media may be used to sustain the position of any holder of power anywhere in the system; they may be used as effectively against an administration as on behalf of one" (1963: 16). The government, on the other hand, may seek to suppress information, plant stories with friendly journalists, or engage in "deliberate leaks" to get its point across. But both are able to justify their actions in terms of a public mandate. The media point to their obligation to provide the "truth" to the public as a crucial part of the democratic process. Those in government, however, point with equal vigor to their obligation to lead the country; an obligation which demands that they be able to take their case to the American people through the media. Both interpretations are well founded.

In fact, as should be evident by now, many of the apparent contradictions among these different perceptions of the relationship among government, media, and public opinion are no more than different perspectives on the same phenomenon. In much the same manner as that reflected in the story of the three blind men trying to describe an elephant, each of these impressions has an element of truth, but none of them has captured the whole picture. The view of the media as "information conduits" supporting the democratic process by informing the public is valid if for no other reason than the fact that many government and public leaders believe in it and act based upon those beliefs. The language in the previously quoted passage from NSC-68 is ample testimony to this fact. The concept of "agenda setting" is also an important aspect of the relationship, but it is clearly a role shared by the government and the media. The media has the power to decide what stories are important: the government has the power to create the stories. In this same vein, the government does seem to have the initiative in providing leadership for public opinion. Such initiative may be viewed as "manipulation" by some, but it is constrained by the fact that there are other voices which also have access to the public through the mass media. What is needed, it would appear, is some framework which attempts to bring all of these elements together so that the completed picture looks more like an "elephant," and less like "a snake, a rope, and a tree."

A preliminary effort at such a framework should begin by recognizing that the relative influence of the government (and in particular the executive branch), the mass media, and public opinion vary considerably, depending upon the point in the foreign policy decision-making process at which they are considered.[2] Most foreign policy decisions are founded upon perceptions of events or situations in the international environment which are interpreted as either providing an opportunity for furthering the "national interests" or demanding a response to protect those interests. At the early stages in this process, much of the initiative is clearly with the government, which may in fact be the initial source of "news" of the external event to the media.[3]

Once an event is perceived, both the government and the media need to apply some interpretation to its significance: the government, from the point of view of the "national interests" (which may include the effect of the event on public support for government positions); the media from the perspective of whether or not the event is newsworthy. Again, the government plays a significant role in the media decision, for if a government spokesman describes an event as significant, it is a virtual certainty that the government statement will receive news coverage. Thus both the government and the media play a role in setting the agenda for public discussion. Where conflict between the governmental and media agendas emerges, it is usually not because the government is unable to get its items on the media agenda, but because other sources have provided the media with significant agenda items that are competing with those desired by the administration.

Note that the mass public has not been mentioned until this point. That is because, as has been previously noted, the public is unlikely to find out about a foreign affairs event until the media has interpreted it as newsworthy. While it is clearly possible for the government to reach certain opinion elites directly, to mobilize mass public opinion the media are indispensable. As a result, the setting of the public agenda is a process which involves the perception and interpretation of events by both the government and the media. Moreover, the setting of an agenda for public discussion does not occur in a vacuum. Agenda items are not written on a blank slate. Room must be found for them among any number of other items which have already been placed on the agenda by government and media action. Thus, by the time the government's agenda is presented to the public, it may be in competition not only with other agenda items selected by the press, but with previous items presented to the public by the government as well.

The conflict which can result from such a situation becomes particularly apparent at the next stage of the foreign policy process, as the government attempts to develop a response to the perceived event. If the public agenda and governmental agenda are in agreement at this point, then the administration can use its public support both as an internal tool to secure bipartisan backing for its recommendations, and as an instrument of international relations to provide added credibility to its position. If, however, the two agendas are out of synchronization with one another, the public demands for action on previous or competing agenda items may pose serious problems for administration attempts to formulate and implement its policy options.

For some policy options, the need for public support may be seen by the administration as minimal. In these cases, as long as the government's policy is not portrayed as being directly contrary to the "will of the people," it may be possible for the administration to proceed on its own. In most cases, however, the administration will need at least a minimum level of support in order to get its program through Congress or to convince the leaders of other countries that its intentions are serious. Faced with such a situation, the initiative clearly lies with the government to "sell" its policy in such a manner that the public demands are modified or satisfied. Only then will an effective policy response prove feasible. Such was clearly the case with NSC-68.

II. NSC-68 AND CONFLICTING AGENDAS

As the presidential directive formally initiating the process of drafting NSC-68 indicated, the proximate cause of this policy review was the explosion of the first Soviet atomic bomb in the latter half of 1949 (Johnson, 1983: 956).[4] On September 23, 1949, President Truman, noting that he was prompted by the belief that "the American people . . . are entitled to be informed," announced to the media that "we have evidence that within recent weeks an atomic explosion occurred in the USSR" (Public Papers, 1949: 485). The thrust of his announcement was that the explosion had not taken the government by surprise, and that there was no immediate cause for alarm. "The eventual development of this new force by other nations was to be expected," he stated. "This probability has always been taken into account by us" (*ibid*).

This same theme was echoed by spokesmen from throughout the administration. Secretary of State Acheson, in a statement released the same day, reiterated the President's comments almost verbatim, emphasizing that virtually every public statement by the administration on atomic weapons had "clearly pointed out that this situation would develop," and stressing that "this event makes no change in our policy" (State: 3 Oct 1949: 487). Such statements were dutifully reported by the news media in the following days. Typical was this comment in the *New York Times* on the 24th of September:

> Privately as well as publicly, high civilian and mili-
> tary officials were calm and reassuring. In no quarter was
> there any hint of dismay. . . . General Omar Bradley, chair-
> man of the Joint Chiefs of Staff, expressed the official
> tone and demeanor in this statement: 'The calmer the

American people take this the better. We have antici-
pated it for four years, and it calls for no change in our
basic defense plan (NYT, 24 Sep. 1949: 2A).

In fact, of over a dozen articles on the front pages of the *New
York Times* and the *Washington Post* which dealt with the explosion the day after the presidential announcement, only one story
noted that the real significance was not the fact that the Soviets
had developed a bomb, but the *timing* of that development. As the
headlines over a by-lined column by William Laurence noted, the
"Soviet Achievement was Ahead of Predictions by 3 Years" (NYT,
24 Sep., 1949: 1A). "It had been customary," he accurately reported,
"to refer to 1952 as possibly the year when Russia would reach the
stage we were at in the summer of 1945." Despite General Bradley's
call for calm, Laurence was alarmed by the implications of this
new situation. As he put it:

> It would be dangerous to assume that they are four
> years behind us and that it would take them that long to
> catch up with us. It would be much more reasonable to
> assume that they have geared their plants to produce at a
> rate of one bomb a week, so that they will have a stock-
> pile of at least 50 bombs a year from now, enough to
> destroy 50 of our cities with 40,000,000 of our population.

It was precisely this sort of interpretation that the administration wished to avoid putting on the Soviet explosion, because to do
so placed an item on the public agenda that was in direct competition with the basic governmental agenda in 1949. In particular, the
Truman administration was publicly committed to the concept of a
balanced budget, and an austere defense budget was a central
element in its efforts. In response to presidential pressure to avoid
either higher taxes or budget deficits, the initial drafts of the
administration's fiscal year 1951 budget circulating in the summer
of 1949 had placed a $13.5 billion ceiling on defense spending
(Acheson, 1969: 452). Moreover, the administration was already
making plans for an even smaller defense budget in following
years. As General Bradley explained in testimony before the House
Armed Services Committee in October of 1949, over a month *after*
the announcement of the Soviet atomic explosion: "We realize that
our nation's economy, under existing conditions, can afford only a

limited amount for defense, and that we must look forward to diminishing appropriations for the armed services" (quoted in Huntington, 1961: 49-50).

There was clearly no room in the agenda being pushed by the administration for a massive increase in defense spending to compensate for the loss of the American atomic monopoly. In fact, as late as spring of 1950, as NSC-68 was nearing completion, the President was still publicly defending a reduced defense budget. In an early March press conference, he responded to criticism that "economies in the Defense Department have weakened our defenses dangerously" by asserting: "I don't think there is a word of truth in it. . . . I think you will find that the national defense situation is in better shape than it has ever been in times when we were not at war" (Public Papers, 1950: 183).

That such criticisms were being raised at presidential press conferences, however, clearly points to a marked difference between the government's public agenda and the agenda being put forward by representatives of the mass media at this time.[5] This shift in the media agenda, which had been partially foretold by the Laurence article in the *New York Times* in September of 1949, had begun gathering momentum within a few weeks of the announcement of the Soviet explosion. On the 3rd of October, an editorial in *Life* magazine called upon the government to "recognize that Soviet possession of the bomb justifies a completely new approach to security" (3 Oct 1949: 22). A week later, to emphasize the point, *Life* ran an article entitled "Can Russia Deliver the Bomb?" which asserted that it was already feasible for the Soviets to attack the United States with nuclear weapons by sneaking them into American ports aboard merchant ships (10 Oct 1949: 44).[6] To illustrate their article, the editors ran a 1920 photograph of a terrorist bomb attack on Wall Street which they attributed to "Reds," despite the fact that no link between the 1920 explosion and Communists was ever demonstrated (Aronson, 1970: 57).

That the media agenda was having an effect on the public is evident from the concern expressed by those within the government during this period. By February of 1950, for example, George Kennan felt compelled to write a memo to Dean Acheson outlining his views "in light of the current demand in the Congress and the press that we re-evaluate our entire policy" (FRUS, 1950 Vol. I: 160-167). Kennan was concerned that the media were exaggerating the threat. "The overall situation," he asserted, "while serious, is neither unexpected nor necessarily catastrophic." What was serious, he believed, was the apparent inability of the government to present its own agenda in a manner which would win public acceptance. There was a need "to improve our general impact on press and Congress and public." Unless this need was met, he saw a "serious and urgent danger that our present policy toward the Soviet Union will founder on the lack of popular support." To prevent such an outcome, he observed that:

> I think it quite essential that we find a new and much more effective approach to the problem of making our policies understood within this Government and among our own people.... Up to this time, it seems to me, we have been quite unsuccessful in this. You still have the most distinguished and influential of our columnists and diplomatic observers making statements which reflect an almost incredible ignorance of the basic elements of our foreign policy, to say nothing of the state of mind of Congressional circles (FRUS, 1950 Vol. I: 166).

Kennan was not the only member of the State Department to express his concern about the impact of public opinion on the administration's policies during this period. Less than one week after the press conference in which President Truman defended the low levels of defense spending, Edward Barrett, Assistant Secretary of State for Public Affairs, circulated a memorandum in which he observed that "talks with a number of Congressmen in the last few days, who have told me about their mail, underscores my belief that there is increasing public pressure, which could become dangerous, for some sort of bold action" (FRUS, 1950 Vol. I: 185).

Such calls for bold action, it should be noted, were not falling on totally deaf ears within the administration. While George Kennan was concerned that the Soviet threat was being exaggerated, Dean Acheson was worried that it was not being stated forcefully enough. The Secretary of State had long been a supporter of a more forceful defense posture toward the Soviet Union, and had in fact been one of the prime movers behind efforts to get the President to authorize a study such as NSC-68 (Acheson, 1969: 451–457). Now, as the document neared completion, he was fully aware of its potential as a public relations tool. As such, he believed there was a need to overstate the nature of the threat.

> The task of a public officer seeking to explain and gain support for a major policy is not that of the writer of a doctoral thesis. Qualification must give way to simplicity of statement, nicety and nuance to bluntness, almost brutality, in carrying home a point (1969: 489).

Acheson was aware that it was not just to the public that he would have to sell the arguments of NSC-68. The administration and the Congress would have to be sold as well, during a period of what Acheson described as "partisan in-fighting as bloody as any in our history" (1969: 451). The course of action required to carry through with the recommendations of the study would represent a total reversal from the policies that had been advocated by the administration through the early part of 1950. Rather than fiscal restraint and a tight defense budget, NSC-68 would require a massive increase in defense spending supported by higher tax rates and a Keynesian view of economic management (Gaddis, 1982: 93–94). In the words of the document itself:

> A program for rapidly building up strength and improving political and economic conditions will place heavy demands on our courage and intelligence; it will be costly; it will be dangerous. But half measures will be more costly and more dangerous, for they will be inadequate to prevent and may actually invite war. Budgetary considerations will need to be subordinated to the stark fact that our very independence as a nation may be at stake (NSC-68, in FRUS 1950, Vol. I: 285).

The document goes on to urge "increases in expenditures for military purposes.... in military assistance programs.... [and] in economic assistance programs." These increases are to be supported by "reduction of Federal expenditures for purposes other than defense and foreign assistance, if necessary by the deferment of certain desirable programs," and through "increased taxes" (*ibid*). NSC-68 itself did not contain any specific cost estimates, but as Acheson notes, "that did not mean we had not discussed them." The opinion of the State-Defense Policy Review Group was that meeting the requirements imposed by the NSC-68 recommendations would involve "a military budget of the magnitude of about fifty billion dollars" (Acheson, 1969: 491).

While the public and media agendas during the early months of 1950 were clearly moving in the direction of a stronger military response to a growing Soviet threat, there is little evidence to suggest that public opinion was prepared for a shift of anything like the magnitude contemplated in NSC-68. In fact, on the 6th of March, 1950, the State Department Office of Public Affairs issued a "Confidential" report on "American Public Attitudes toward Possible Adoption of Stronger U.S. Foreign Policy Measures" which indicated just how far public opinion would have to be moved to win acceptance for such a program (FRUS 1950, Vol. I: 185). Based on "extensive study of public comment in press and radio, of the positions taken by major national organizations, and of the findings of public opinion surveys," the report concluded that although "the overwhelming majority of Americans believe that the United States must continue its efforts to stop Communist expansion," resistance could be expected to any proposals requiring "personal sacrifice. . . . new burdens. . . . higher taxes and a more unbalanced budget" (FRUS 1950, Vol. I: 186–187). Of course, these were exactly the sort of sacrifices being called for in NSC-68.

Moreover, in the face of its previous public commitment to hold down defense spending and the evidence that the public was not prepared for a major shift in budgetary priorities, Acheson was aware that it would prove difficult to get the administration itself committed to full endorsement of NSC-68. His fears in this regard seem more than born out by the fact that as late as May 4th, after he had already seen and endorsed the basic concepts of NSC-68, President Truman went on record as stating that "the defense budget next year will be *smaller* than it is this year" (Public Papers, 1950: 286). Little wonder then that Dean Acheson believed that the primary need for NSC-68 was to "so bludgeon the mass mind of 'top government' that not only could the President make a decision, but that the decision could be carried out" (Acheson, 1969: 488).

III. PACKAGING THE PROGRAM

As John Lewis Gaddis has noted, "one of the things most striking about NSC-68 was its rhetorical tone. Portions of it sounded as though they had been intended for the floor of Congress, or some other conspicuous public platform" (1982: 107). In fact, they had been, despite the fact that the overall document remained classified until 1975. What was needed in a statement of policy such as NSC-68, according to Secretary of State Acheson, was "communicable wisdom" (1969: 455).

The general consensus, as reflected in the statement already quoted from George Kennan's memo of 17 February, was that the record of the Department of State in generating "communicable wisdom" up to that point was not particularly outstanding. In the drafting of NSC-68, therefore, Acheson and the members of the State-Defense Policy Review Group spent considerable time attempting to assess how their recommendations could be made understandable to the "mythical 'average American citizen' " who "might spend at most ten minutes a day concerning himself with foreign affairs" (Acheson, 1969: 489; Thompson, 1981: 165).

This task was made more difficult by the fact that the threat to which NSC-68 was addressed was not an immediate one. According to the members of the Policy Review Group, the chief danger from the Soviet Union was believed to be some four years in the future. However, it could only be successfully met if America began rearming herself immediately. The crucial question then became how to sell the administration, Congress, and the public on an expensive and long term program of rearmament which was designed primarily to meet a danger which would not be real until 1954 (Huntington, 1961: 52). The answer was, in effect, to oversell the threat, or to use Acheson's own words, to "make our points clearer than truth" (Acheson, 1969: 489).

The language of NSC-68 itself clearly reflects this decision. Asserting that "the idea of freedom is the most contagious idea in history," it warned that that idea was nevertheless in danger because "the Soviet Union . . . animated by a new fanatic faith, antithetical to our own . . . seeks to impose its absolute authority over the rest of the world" (NSC-68, in FRUS 1950, Vol I: 237). Moreover, the Soviet Union was portrayed as "developing the military capacity to support its design for world domination." Already it was seen to have the capability of overrunning Western Europe, launching air attacks against Britain, and attacking selected targets in the United States with atomic weapons (*ibid:* 249). By 1954, if the Soviet buildup were met with "no more effective defense opposition than the United States and its allies have programmed," a surprise attack could "lay waste to the British Isles" and "devastate . . . vital centers of the United States and Canada" (*ibid:* 251–52).

In response to such challenges, NSC-68 charged that "it is clear that a substantial and rapid buildup of strength in the free world is necessary to support a firm policy intended to check and roll back the Kremlin's drive for world domination." In particular, what was required was "a build-up of military strength by the United States and its allies to a point at which the combined strength will be superior . . . both initially and throughout a war, to the forces that can be brought to bear by the Soviet Union and its satellites" (*ibid:* 283–84). In addition to its military implications, it was necessary to pursue such a course of action to avoid seeing our allies "become increasingly reluctant to support a firm foreign policy on our part." A military build-up was thus seen as necessitated for its "psychological impact—the revival of confidence and hope in the future" (*ibid*: 284).

Faced with the threat of Communist world domination and loss of hope in the future, the cost of the programs required to support the policy recommendations of NSC-68 would seem like a bargain. The crux of the matter, then, was to set the agenda in those terms. As the conclusion to NSC-68 succinctly put it:

> The whole success of the proposed program hangs ultimately on recognition by this Government, the American people, and all free peoples, that the cold war is in fact a real war in which the survival of the free world is at stake. Essential prerequisites to success are consultations with Congressional leaders designed to make the program the subject of non-partisan legislative support, and *a presentation to the public of a full explanation of the facts and implications of the present international situation* (*ibid:* 292, emphasis added).

Preparation for this "presentation to the public" was underway well before the final draft of NSC-68 was completed. Throughout the month of March in 1950, the Policy Review Group held hearings with key citizens who were currently outside of government circles for the express purpose of getting advice on how the basic tenets of NSC-68 might best be "sold" to the American people. These citizen consultants were drawn from a segment of the population that might accurately be described as "opinion elites." Most had held government positions at some point in their careers. Now their task was to review existing drafts of NSC-68 and make recommendations as to how its arguments might be presented in such a way as to have the maximum desired impact on the public.

One of the first of these consultants to advise the Policy Review Group was Chester Barnard, President of the Rockefeller Foundation. His views on the problems facing the Group closely paralleled the earlier observations of George Kennan. "At the present time," he said, "those who do most of the talking do not know the facts" (Record of the Meeting of the State-Defense Policy Review Group, March 10, 1950, in FRUS 1950, Vol. I: 191). He observed that "cohesion in our Democracy is basic to United States security, and that the government was going to need assistance in getting public support for the national effort which would be called for." This, he believed, would be "a difficult job for the government to handle alone" (*ibid*). He felt that the government should seek help from the civilian sector in selling its message to the public. As the minutes of the meeting at which he spoke record:

> Specifically, he advocated setting up a group of five or ten worthy citizens of good reputation and high integrity who have no connection with the government, who would have available to them all of the material on which the government based its conclusions, and who could then say to the people, 'We are thoroughly advised and you can accept what we say' (*ibid*).

Mr. Barnard's conclusions were given a strong endorsement in an independent set of recommendations put forward by former Under Secretary of State Robert Lovett.[7] In a meeting of the Policy Review Group on the 16th of March, Mr. Lovett testified that "he agreed with the general conclusion that we must build up our strength, and he said that this requires, in the first instance, giving the facts to the public" (FRUS 1950: 196). Toward this end, he noted that the NSC document itself contained "some portions which are excellent material for speeches," and suggested that the conclusions should be stated "simply, clearly, and in almost telegraphic style" in what he referred to as "Hemingway sentences" (*ibid*: 197).

Even with a strongly worded document, however, Lovett felt

that the administration was going to face "a terrible problem of public information and support." What was needed, he believed, was a "much vaster propaganda machine to tell our story at home and abroad" (*ibid:* 198–99). As an initial step in this direction, the minutes record that he made several specific suggestions, to include:

> (1) that we get in what he called a 'group of para-phrasers' who could turn what it is we have to say to the American people into understandable terms for the aver-age man on the street. (2) that we parcel out our message to a number of the best speakers in the Government to be reiterated and reiterated and reiterated. (3) we should enlist the aid of schools, colleges, churches, and other groups. . . . (4) he suggested that we get a group of elder statesmen (very much like that suggested by Mr. Barnard) which would "audit and certify" our findings and thereby back up the Administration's statement of the facts (FRUS 1950, Vol. I: 199–200. Parenthetical phrase in the original).

That considerations such as these were being solicited as part of the process of drafting NSC-68 is excellent testimony to the degree to which the document was intended to be "communicable." Of even more striking significance is the fact that almost all of these recommendations were eventually brought into play as the government moved to adopt the policies called for in NSC-68.

It is worth noting that not all of the recommendations for "selling" NSC-68 to the public came from consultants outside of the government. Although his recommendations seem to have been made at a rather late stage in the development of the document (April 6, just one day before the final product was submitted to President Truman for his approval!), the observations of Assist-ant Secretary of State for Public Affairs Edward Barrett are worth serious consideration. Rather than confining himself to the short term tactics of presenting the NSC-68 proposals to the American people, he was concerned with the long term implications of the policies necessary to support those proposals when he wrote:

> My most important point: the whole paper seems to me to point to a gigantic armament race, a huge buildup of conventional arms that quickly become obsolescent, a greatly expanded military establishment in being. I think

that, however much we whip up sentiment, we are going
to run into vast opposition among informed people to a
huge arms race.... Moreover, even if we should sell the
idea, I fear that the U.S. public would rapidly tire of such
an effort. In the absence of a real and continuing crisis, a
dictatorship can unquestionably out-last a democracy in
a conventional armament race (FRUS 1950: 225).

Such reservations notwithstanding, Barrett observed that he
considered the overall document "a magnificent job of analyzing
the problem," and he believed in the need to educate the public
about its contents. "If and when this whole project is approved by
the President," he stated, "the public education campaign must
obviously receive the most careful study." He was concerned,
however, lest the selling of the threat generate pressure for steps
which the government might not be prepared to take.

"We must be sure," he cautioned, "that the Government is in a position to come forward with positive steps
to be taken just as soon as the atmosphere is right. It is
imperative, for both domestic and overseas reasons, that
there should not be too much of a time lag between the
creation of a public awareness of the problem and the
setting forth of a positive Government program to solve
that problem.
"In other words, we should have at least the broad
proposals for action well in hand before the psychological
'scare campaign' is started" (FRUS 1950, Vol. I: 226).

Whether as a "psychological scare campaign" or a "bludgeon"
for the "mass mind of the top government," NSC-68 was clearly
intended to place the rearmament of the Western world at the top
of the government and public agendas for action. On April 7, 1950,
the State-Defense Policy Review Group submitted it to President
Truman for approval. On April 12th, he referred it to the National
Security Council "for consideration, with the request that [the
Council] provide me with further information on the implications
of the Conclusions contained therein.... including estimates of
the probable cost of such programs" (FRUS 1950, Vol. I: 235).

The probable cost of such programs, as has already been
indicated, was one of the critical stumbling blocks in the path of

gaining full administration approval for NSC-68. While some accounts, including Dean Acheson's own, indicate that NSC-68 had become national policy by the end of April (Acheson, 1969: 488), the fact that the President was still publicly committed to further reductions in defense spending in early May casts some doubt on how fully he was willing to support the Policy Review Group's proposals. Truman does not appear to have been alone in his reservations on this matter, for as late as June 5th of 1950, Secretary of Defense Louis Johnson was still saying that he did not expect defense costs to be increased (Gaddis, 1982: 113).

While others in the administration may not have been sure about endorsing the recommendations of NSC-68 as national policy, there was no doubt in Dean Acheson's mind. Throughout the spring of 1950, he went about the country "preaching the premise of NSC-68," as he put it, in a series of public speeches and appearances before Congressional committees (Acheson, 1969: 489; Gaddis, 1982: 108). By early June, President Truman had also begun to talk in terms of "a program that will create the greatest possible national strength" (Public Papers, 1950: 457). Still, he had not yet officially endorsed NSC-68 and its full range of policy recommendations.[8] As a result, the overall impression left by the administration through most of the spring was that of a government unsure of its own course in national defense.

This confusion as to what was actually on the national agenda was reflected as well in the agenda being presented in the mass media throughout the same time period. A series of articles and editorials in *U.S. News and World Report* during May of 1950 will serve to illustrate the point. On May 5th, a full page editorial by David Lawrence urged the government to hold down defense spending, noting that Russia was "trying to bleed the U.S. to death in an arms race." (USNWR, 5 May 1950: 52). On the 19th, however, an article in the "Tomorrow" section observed that "Russia, to date, is gaining in the arms race," and called on the United States to "speed up." "A cold war cannot be fought without danger," it noted, and continued by asserting that "danger can't well be faced without a strong defense . . . Defense, in turn, costs money, lots of it, much more, probably, than the U.S. is spending now" (USNWR, 19 May 1950: 7). The next week, the cover story asked the question: "Can Russia Defeat the U.S.?", and answered by stating that "Stalin's chances of winning an early war are slipping away," due to the stockpile of American atomic weapons (USNWR, 26 May 1950: cover, 16).

Whether or not the "psychological scare campaign" envisioned by Edward Barrett or the use of NSC-68 as a "bludgeon" in Acheson's hands would have eventually proved sufficient to bring order to this confused agenda will probably never be known, for on June 24th, 1950, communist forces halfway around the globe provided a bludgeon of their own by invading South Korea. Acheson himself gives a considerable amount of credit to the invasion as the prime force behind the adoption of NSC-68, noting that " . . . it is doubtful that anything like what happened in the next few years could have been done had not the Russians been stupid enough to have instigated the attack against South Korea" (1969: 488). Edward Barrett was even more blunt in his assessment. Noting the problems faced in getting the administration to unite behind NSC-68 throughout the spring, he stated: "We were sweating over it, and then . . . thank God, Korea came along" (quoted in Nathan & Oliver, 1981: 118).

IV. SELLING THE POLICY

While a great deal can be said for the point of view that the Korean War provided the impetus needed to move massive rearmament to the top of the administration's agenda for action, it would be a serious overstatement to claim that this assured the success of NSC-68. To be sure, one of the most tangible immediate effects of the invasion of South Korea was an administration request for a $10 billion increase in its defense authorizations for FY 1951. In fact, this represented only the first of four such requests (designated NSC-68/1 through NCS-68/4) between July and December of 1950, the cumulative effect of which was to raise the total amount asked for defense from the original $13.5 billion to $48.2 billion by the year's end (Gaddis, 1982: 113).

Nevertheless, NSC-68 had been based on an assumption of strengthening America's overall global military posture toward the Soviet Union, not just fighting a police action on an Asian peninsula. The willingness of Congress to appropriate money for defense during a time of overt hostilities with Communist forces did not necessarily equate to a willingness to support the sort of long range build up of forces-in-being envisioned by the Policy Review Group, as debate over administration policies through the first quarter of 1951 was to prove. As had been noted in a memo by Assistant Deputy Secretary of State Llewellyn Thompson in April of 1950, "if the conclusions [of NSC-68] are to be carried out, they would have to ... have the full support not only of the administration, but of the Congress and public as well" (FRUS 1950, Vol. I: 214). Korea may have won the battle within the administration, but it only set the stage for the fight in the other two arenas.

In the Congress, opposition by Republican leaders committed to reduced government spending and fewer overseas commitments threatened to block the allocation of men, money, and material which would be necessary to support the programs of NSC-68. In particular, two key proposals came to represent the focal point of conflict over the implementation of NSC-68 in what was termed the "Great Debate" on Truman's foreign policy: an increase by four divisions (from two to six) in the number of U.S. troops permanently based in Europe; and the authorization of a $7.5 billion economic and military assistance package under the terms of the Mutual Security Act of 1951 (Congressional Quarterly Almanac, 1951: 204, 220; Sanders, 1983: 86–88).

Not surprisingly, the battle in the Congress set the tone for the battle for public support, as the administration sought to build public willingness to support the militarization of containment through both higher taxes and increased military service. Unfortunately for the supporters of NSC-68, not only did they face conservative Republican opposition on both of these issues, but both were policies to which the administration had itself been strongly opposed just the year before. It was, as one study put it, "a classical case where the aims of foreign policy ... run up against the constraints of domestic politics" (Sanders, 1983: 62). It was, however, with an eye toward overcoming just such constraints that NSC-68 had been drafted in the first place.

By December of 1950, the rhetoric of NSC-68 was clearly in evidence as President Truman went before the American people in a national radio and television broadcast to declare a state of national emergency. "I am talking to you tonight," he began, "about what our country is up against:"

Our homes, our Nation, all the things we believe in
are in great danger. This danger has been created by the
rulers of the Soviet Union. . . . The future of civilization
depends on what we do—on what we do now, and in the
months ahead. . . . All of us will have to pay more taxes
and do without things we like. . . . [because] measured
against the danger that confronts us, our forces are not
adequate. . . . We must . . . work with the other free nations
to strengthen our combined defenses . . . build up our
own Army, Navy, and Air Force, and make more weapons
for ourselves and our allies (Public Papers, 1950: 741-746).

While the President was able to make a strong case by drawing
on the concepts of NSC-68, he was hampered to some extent in
getting his message across by the fact that the debate had strong
partisan overtones. Unless some sort of bipartisan support could
be built for the administration's proposals, there were no guarantees
that the public would be willing to make the sort of sacrifices the
President was calling for. After all, as one news magazine had
noted earlier in the year, "the Cold War tends to heat up . . . each
year at about the time that Congress is getting ready to decide the
size of military appropriations" (USNWR, 14 Apr 1950: 8). To
many people, even in the context of the ongoing war in Korea, a
large part of the debate over NSC-68 must have looked like "politics
as usual."

Fortunately for the cause of the administration, the creation of
the needed bipartisan support had in fact already begun, its seeds
sown in the March recommendations of Chester Barnard and
Robert Lovett that the government might be helped in its campaign by a panel of "worthy citizens" who "had not been tarred
with the Administration's brush in the eyes of the people" (FRUS
1950, Vol. I: 199-200). In his March testimony, Barnard had
mentioned the possibility that someone like James B. Conant, the
President of Harvard University, would make a fitting member of
such a group (ibid: 191). In August of 1950, Conant was approached
by Tracy Voorhees, who was a member of the National Security
Council's Ad Hoc Committee in charge NSC-68's planning, with
the proposal that he "get a group of distinguished citizens together,
draw up a program, put it before the public, get people to write
Congress and, in general, respond to the gravity of the situation"

(Sanders, 1983: 61). Conant, who had himself been one of the citizen consultants who reviewed NSC-68 for the Policy Review Group, was attracted to the idea, but noted that such a group "could be effective only if it were welcomed (unofficially but sincerely) by the administration" (Conant, 1970: 335).

In September of 1950, Robert Lovett himself re-entered government service as Deputy Secretary of Defense, and it was he whom Tracy Voorhees approached to arrange such an "unofficial but sincere" welcome. Not surprisingly, given his own call for the creation of just such a group only months before, Lovett was enthusiastic, and suggested that Secretary of Defense Marshall be made aware of the group's plans. Conant subsequently drafted a letter to the Secretary on behalf of the group which succinctly stated their purpose: "Specifically, we have thought that one way in which such a committee might be of help would be in strengthening the public support for such stern measures as may be necessary" (Sanders, 1983: 66). When Marshall responded in late November by giving his endorsement to what he termed "an undertaking of great importance," it was decided that the time was ripe for the group to publicly announce its existence and intentions (*ibid:* 67).

Thus it was that on December 13th, 1950, just two days prior to President Truman's declaration of a state of emergency, the front page of the *New York Times* announced the creation of the Committee on the Present Danger, described by the *Times'* reporter as being "composed of twenty-five leaders in American life . . . including leading scientists and educators" (NYT, 13 Dec 1950: 1, 19). In its own statement, reprinted in full by the *Times,* the Committee described itself as having been "formed in the American tradition by civilians acting on a nonpartisan basis" (*ibid:* 19). Clearly the group of "worthy citizens" who would provide independent support for the administration's endorsement of NSC-68 had arrived.

The statement issued by the Committee that day set the tone for most of its subsequent announcements. Not surprisingly, given the close association of its founders with the basic document, sections of the Committee's press release appeared to be paraphrased almost directly from arguments in NSC-68 itself.

> The aggressive designs of the Soviet Union are unmistakably plain. . . . Unless an adequate support for

the atomic potential of the United States is brought into existence, the time may soon come when all of Continental Europe can be forced into the Communist fold.

In our view, the necessary support ... is an allied force in being strong enough to furnish effective resistance to military aggression. . . . That force does not exist. To meet the need, it must be promptly built. To create it, the United States must take the leadership. Our part will call for greater sacrifices than any our people have yet been prepared for. . . . It will render necessary a sharp reduction in Government spending for non-defense purposes.

The doubt is not whether such a program is too arduous. The doubt is whether it is arduous enough. Certainly it is not nearly as drastic as the conditions which make it necessary. The price is high, but we believe it must be paid (NYT, 13 Dec 1950: 19).

The arrival on the scene of Lovett's "group of paraphrasers" could not have come at a better time from the Truman administration's point of view. On December 20th, former President Herbert Hoover fired a strong opening salvo in the "Great Debate" on the Truman national security program by issuing a "demand for a new foreign policy" in a nationwide radio and television broadcast. In it, he called for virtual abandonment of Western Europe and a retrenchment to "preserve this Western Hemisphere Gibraltar" through reducing expenses and balancing the budget (NYT, 21 Dec 1950: 1, 22). Significantly, on the page facing the one on which they ran the text of ex-President Hoover's statement, the *Times* ran a rebuttal of that statement by Committee on the Present Danger member Robert Patterson (*ibid:* 21).

In January of 1951, President Truman provided his own rejoinder to those who were "whispering of a return to isolationism" in the form of his State of the Union Address to Congress. As with his national emergency speech, it was evident that the concepts of NSC-68 formed the core of his arguments: "The threat of world conquest by Soviet Russia endangers our liberty and endangers the kind of world in which the free spirit of man can survive," he began, echoing almost directly the "hope of the future" theme of NSC-68. He continued in a similar vein, noting that:

The imperialism of the czars has been replaced by an even more ambitious ... crafty ... and menacing imperi-

alism of the rulers of the Soviet Union. This new imperialism has powerful military forces. . . . The present rulers of
the Soviet Union have shown that they are willing to use
this power to destroy the free nations and win domination
over the whole world (Public Papers, 1951: 7).

To meet this threat, the President called upon Congress to
reject partisan rivalries and "stand together as Americans" in support of administration programs which would "give priority to
activities that are urgent—like military procurement," while prac-
ticing "rigid economy in its non-defense activities" (*ibid:* 12–13). As
the Congressional session got underway, however, Republican attacks
on the proposals to send additional troops to Europe and the
Mutual Security Act funding levels made it clear that such bi-partisan
support was not to be found in the legislative branch.

As the debate in Congress heated up, so did the activities of the
Committee on the Present Danger. Throughout the early months
of 1951, the Committee issued a series of press statements stressing
the group's non-partisan nature and urging the public to support
the administration's position. As far as can be determined, every
statement released by the Committee received full coverage in the
media, with the *New York Times* frequently giving them headlines
on the front page.[9] Typical was the page one article generated by
their press conference the day after the President's State of the
Union Address, which the *Times* featured in part because it "came
at a time when the nation's foreign policy was being debated, both
in the new Eighty-second Congress and in forums elsewhere in the
country" (NYT, 8 Jan 1951: 1). Calling specifically for support on
sending troops to NATO, the statement read, in part:

> On these problems, the Committee on the Present
> Danger ventures, completely without partisanship, to pres-
> ent its deeply held convictions.
> Certain facts are beyond dispute:
> A menacing despotic power, bent on conquering the
> world, has twice in recent months in Korea resorted to
> aggression. . . . Europe is the next great prize Russia seeks
> (NYT, 8 Jan 1951: 7).

The first week in March, the Committee stepped up its activities,
beginning a series of weekly nationwide radio broadcasts over the

Mutual Broadcasting System (NYT, 5 Mar 1951: 1). By this time, the Committee consisted of approximately 45 members, many of whom were frequent guests at State Department and Pentagon briefing sessions in Washington, in which they were afforded access to classified information including NSC-68 and its supporting documents. This information was extensively used in support of the Committee's broadcasts (Sanders, 1983: 93). In fact, as an extensive study of their activities during this period put it,

> The Committee's concern was how, and to what extent, to go public with NSC-68. The idea was to squeeze the isolationist diehards between the Administration and a popular groundswell. If successful, this strategy would isolate the isolationists from their crucial base of support in mass opinion (Sanders, 1983: 90).

The strategy appears to have worked, for on the fourth of April, one month after the broadcasts began, the three month long Senate debate on sending troops to Europe came to an end with a successful 69–21 vote for the administration position (Congressional Quarterly Almanac, 1951: 220). It had not been quite as easy as the size of the vote makes it appear, however. An attempt to get an identically worded concurrent resolution through both the House and Senate passed the Senate by only 45–41, and failed to even reach a vote in the House (*ibid*). Although debate on the foreign military and economic aid package in the Mutual Security Act continued on into the fall, by the first week in October the administration had won that battle in both the House and Senate as well (*ibid*: 211). From this point on, NSC-68 can be considered to have been, without question, American national policy. The governmental, media, and public agendas were all in agreement, and the concept of military containment of the Soviet Union was not seriously questioned again until the 1960s.

The exact degree of influence of any one particular factor in securing the adoption of NSC-68 and the militarization of containment policy is impossible to ascertain. Clearly the outbreak of the Korean War was a factor, as was the intense lobbying effort by those within the administration who supported the premises upon which NSC-68 was founded. To no small extent, however, credit must be given to the manner in which the administration was able to "sell" NSC-68 to the public, both through its own direct efforts and those of its allied opinion elites. As James Conant noted in his memoirs, "I have always cherished the thought that the Committee on the Present Danger, by its statements and the broadcasts of several members, played an important role in shaping public opinion on this issue" (1970: 517).

The question which might reasonably be asked in conclusion, though, is "at what cost?" Walter LaFeber has described NSC-68 as "one of the key historical documents of the Cold War. It asked the United States to assume unilaterally the defense of the free world at a tremendous price and with no hesitation" (1967: 90–91). In a document of such significance, it would not be unreasonable to hope for analysis based upon considered wisdom. But such does not seem to be the case for NSC-68. Indeed, John Lewis Gaddis describes it as "a deeply flawed document," and cites among his reasons for this conclusion the fact that it was primarily a work of advocacy (1982; 106). What are the implications in designing national policy around a document that was in many respects created as a "sales pitch?"

The problem is not a new one. It is, in fact, the basic dilemma which arises out of the need to build public support for foreign policy in a democracy; a dilemma noted by De Tocqueville when he wrote:

> Democracy appears to me better adapted for the conduct of society in times of peace, or for a sudden effort of remarkable vigor, than for the prolonged endurance of the great storms which beset the political existence of nations. . . . Foreign politics demand scarcely any of those qualities which are peculiar to a democracy. . . . [A] democracy can only with great difficulty regulate the details of an important undertaking, persevere in a fixed design, and work out its execution. . . . It cannot combine its measures with secrecy or await their consequences with patience. (1954: 237–244).

It appears to be this same pessimistic outlook of the inability of a democracy to build public support for its foreign policy in a calm and rational manner which runs throughout the framework of NSC-68. Turning once more to the document itself, it laments that "the very virtues of our system . . . handicap us in certain respects," and goes on to the sad conclusion that:

In coping with dictatorial governments acting in secrecy and with speed we are vulnerable in that the democratic process necessarily operates in the open and at a deliberate tempo. Weaknesses in our situation are readily apparent and subject to immediate exploitation. This Government therefore cannot afford in the face of the totalitarian challenge to operate on a narrow margin of strength. A democracy can compensate for its natural vulnerability only if it maintains clearly superior overall power in its most inclusive sense (FRUS 1950, Vol. I: 255).

If such are in fact the beliefs of those who labored to develop NSC-68, there can be little doubt as to why Acheson chose to use a "bludgeon" as his tool for transmitting "communicable wisdom!"

A Framework for Consideration of the Relationships Among Government, Media, and Public Opinion in Developing Policy Responses to International Events

INTERNATIONAL	GOVERNMENTAL	MEDIA	PUBLIC
Action			
	Perception	Perception	
	Interpretation	Interpretation	Perception & Interpretation
	Perception of Need for Response		Public Demand
	Response Initiation		
	Policy Formulation		Demand
		Coverage & Interpretation	Satisfaction Modification
	Policy Implementation		
Reaction			

Source: Author

The model is intended to reflect information and opinion flow in foreign policy decision making in a manner which takes into account the "information conduit," "agenda setting," and "manipulation" models discussed in the text.

Solid lines represent the primary channels of information or opinion flow. Secondary channels are represented by dotted lines.

The categories across the top reflect the different environments within which the agenda setting process occurs. They have been condensed for simplicity of presentation. As the discussion in the text indicates, there are significant distinctions between the different branches of the government, different types of mass media, and different levels of "public" opinion.

It is important to note that the process depicted above does not occur in a vacuum. Actions occurring in the international environment must be perceived against a background of an almost infinite number of other actions occurring simultaneously. This is true for governmental, media and public perceptions. As a result, there is already a relatively full public agenda into which any new perception must be fit. Moreover, actions in the international environment continue throughout the entire process, and may radically alter the nature of the response being considered or the process by which that process is being developed. Such was the case with the invasion of Korea as it related to the "sale" of NSC-68.

NOTES

1. There are studies which show that this situation may be undergoing a significant shift due to the growth in the use of polls which make it easy to read "mass opinion", however uninformed it may be. (See for example Sabato, 1981: 319–321).
2. A flow chart model of the relationship described here may be found in the appendix.
3. This should not obscure the fact that there are many documented cases in which governmental leaders obtained their initial information from media stories. To a degree, this may be a function of where you are in the governmental "chain of command."
4. Most studies also note the "loss" of mainland China to the Communist forces under Mao in 1949 as a causal factor. See, for example, the account by Gaddis which lists China, the Soviet bomb, and internal debates over strategy as being among the "shocks of 1949" which led to the study (1982: 90).
5. I use the term "government's public agenda" here because it is clear that by this time the private opinions of those working on NSC-68 were significantly different from those being articulated by the President.
6. The article also mentioned the possibility of attack by Soviet "Bull" bombers (copies of our B-29) and by rockets fired from submarines off our coasts.
7. Mr. Lovett was soon to be back in government service. He was appointed Deputy Secretary of Defense in September of 1950, at the same time General Marshall was brought in to replace Louis Johnson as Secretary of Defense.
8. Truman officially approved the document on September 30, 1950.

9. Not a particularly surprising finding, given the Committee member-ship of Edward R. Murrow and *New York Times* editor Julius Ochs Adler.

REFERENCES

Acheson, Dean. 1969. *Present at the Creation: My Years in the State Department.* New York: Signet.

Aronson, James. 1970. *The Press and the Cold War.* New York: Bobbs-Merrill.

Cohen, Bernard C. 1963. *The Press and Foreign Policy.* Princeton, N.J.: Princeton University Press.

Conant, James B. 1970. *My Several Lives.* New York: Harper and Row.

Department of State Bulletin. 1949-1951, Volumes 21-23. Washington; U.S. Government Printing Office.

De Tocqueville, Alexis. 1954 edition. *Democracy in America.* New York: Vintage.

Foreign Relations of the United States. 1950, Volume I. Washington: U.S. Government Printing Office (1977).

Gaddis, John Lewis. 1982. *Strategies of Containment.* New York: Oxford University Press.

Graber, Doris A. 1980. *Mass Media and American Politics.* Washington, D.C.: Congressional Quarterly Press.

Huntington, Samuel P. 1961. *The Common Defense.* New York: Columbia University Press.

Johnson, Robert H. 1983. "Periods of Peril: The Window of Vulnerability and Other Myths." *Foreign Affairs* Vol. 61, No. 4 (Spring): 950-970.

LaFeber, Walter. 1967. *America, Russia, and the Cold War, 1945-1966.* New York: John Wiley and Sons.

Life Magazine. 3 October 1949, 10 October 1949.

Nathan, James A., and James K. Oliver. 1981. *United States Foreign Policy and World Order.* Boston: Little, Brown and Company.

_____. 1983. *Foreign Policy Making and the American Political System.* Boston: Little, Brown and Company.

The New York Times. September, 1949-March, 1951. Selected issues.

Paletz, David L., and Robert M. Entman. 1981. *Media—Power—Politics.* New York: The Free Press.

Sabato, Larry J. 1981. *The Rise of Political Consultants.* New York: Basic Books.

Sanders, Jerry W. 1983. *Peddlers of Crisis: The Committee on the Present Danger and the Politics of Containment.* Boston: South End Press.

Thompson, Kenneth W. 1981. *Cold War Theories,* Vol. I. Baton Rouge, Louisiana: LSU Press.

Truman, Harry S. 1949–1950. *Public Papers of the Presidents of the United States.* Washington, D.C.; U.S. Government Printing Office (1965).

U.S. News and World Report. May 5, 19, and 26, 1950.

The Washington Post. 24 September, 1949.

PART TWO

Leadership in
International Law

Making International Law Relevant in the Nuclear Age
BILL PARSONS

I. INTRODUCTION.

One of the most perplexing problems confronting international relations and jurisprudence is the relationship between national security and international law. In an ideal world, of course, there would be only a modest amount of friction between international law and the behavior of nations. The law would codify the accepted and proper activities of states, and the states for their part would adhere to the legal and normative standards set forth. Unfortunately this hope has not been fully realized in recent times. Indeed, given the number of wars and conflicts fought since World War II, the legal norms pertaining to the use of force seem to have been especially victimized. The blunt truth is that we live in a very dangerous world despite the best efforts of the international legal community.

This state of affairs places international lawyers, among others, in an unhappy predicament. As lawyers they must maintain fidelity to the law. Yet as citizens of nation-states they must also serve the best interests of their respective nations whenever possible. The desire to serve the state is particularly intensified when national security concerns are at stake. The result is that lawyers might often perceive a conflict between their fidelity to international law and their duty to promote the security of their nation.

One way to place this potential conflict of interest in perspective is summarized by the "law and national security matrix" shown in Table One. It was initially developed by Professor John Norton Moore at the University of Virginia School of Law. The matrix depicts four possible ways to analyze the relation between a proposed national security action and its legality. Activities undertaken for reasons of national security may be either legal or illegal,

37

permissible or impermissible. Similarly a lawyer or decision-maker may either endorse the proposed action or decide against it. In abstract terms the matrix shows that usually there will not be a conflict between national security and international law. Consider, for example, a proposed overflight of an intelligence reconnaissance aircraft.

One possible situation is depicted in the upper left quadrant of the matrix. Here the proposed action is simply to fly the aircraft over international waters along an accepted air route. This would not be a violation of international law. There is no conflict between international law and national security. As a result, a lawyer or decision-maker would not have any trouble endorsing such an action.

The opposite type of situation is shown in the lower right quadrant. In this case the lawyer is asked about the desirability of shooting down without provocation another country's aircraft while it is flying over international waters. This act would be a patent violation of international law. The lawyer should have no qualms about arguing against such an action.

A more interesting case is displayed in the lower left corner of the matrix. In this situation another nation's aircraft overflies a sensitive military location inside the lawyer's country without prior approval. The intruding aircraft refuses or fails to leave the area. Given these circumstances, under international law the overflown nation could legally use force to bring down the aircraft even though it might entail a large loss of life. The lawyer or decision-maker thus could endorse an action to shoot down the intruder. On the other hand, the nation need not exercise its legal right to do so. Such an act might be permissible but it could also be morally repugnant, particularly if it was clear that the aircraft was unarmed and lost or in mechanical difficulty. This example highlights instances where international law could justify a national security action even though for other reasons it would be ill-considered. It shows that nations need not undertake an activity merely because it would be permissible under international law.

The most perplexing situation, however, involves the one depicted in the upper right quadrant. Here a decision-maker requests advice on whether or not to order an aircraft to violate another nation's airspace in order to obtain badly needed intelligence

TABLE ONE:
The Law and National Security Matrix

Legality of the Proposed Action

		LEGAL	ILLEGAL
	YES	NOT CONTROVERSIAL	VERY CONTROVERSIAL
		Example: order aircraft to fly over international waters	*Example:* order aircraft to overfly another state's territory without permission
Decision Whether To Undertake Proposed Action	**NO**	SOMEWHAT CONTROVERSIAL	NOT CONTROVERSIAL
		Example: decision not to shoot down aircraft intruding into state's own air space	*Example:* decision *not* to shoot down aircraft flying over international waters

information. The act, of course, would be a clear breach of international law.[1] Nonetheless, on the grounds of national security a lawyer or decision-maker might feel compelled to endorse the action. Such a decision, prima facie, would seem to make a mockery out of international law.

This illustration raises a number of interesting questions. First, in general should national security requirements be allowed to override considerations of international law? Second, are there any specific instances where it might be objectively admissible for a state to violate international law in order to promote its national security interests? Third, can a test or analytical framework be fashioned which would enable a decision-maker to make a *principled* and *legitimate* decision to violate a particular legal norm without totally eviscerating international law in the process? These questions will be considered in the remainder of the paper. The next section will discuss whether, as a theoretical matter, national security should ever take precedence over international law.

II. INTERNATIONAL LAW.

Just how one sees the relationship between international law and national security will strongly depend upon one's view of the nature of international law. There are three general ways to characterize international law. Each one will provide a different answer to the question of whether international law should ever be subservient to the interests of national security.

The first approach is to maintain that international law provides an absolute normative framework by which to regulate and evaluate the behavior of nations. Under this view legal norms, being absolute, should never be contravened by considerations of national security. International law should always take precedence over other factors such as military necessity or the national interest. As such there could never be a conflict between international law and national security. The latter must inevitably give way to the former.

One proponent of the "absolutist" view is Tom J. Farer. He maintains that law and morality are the only two legitimate perspectives that are useful for analyzing national behavior.[2] He believes that the national interest can never be of coequal concern with legal norms.[3] For Farer national preference ought not to take precedence over international law.

As a result, when contemplating a national security action, such as intervention in a conflict, the law should not merely be taken into account when formulating a decision. It must be viewed as the final arbiter. To do otherwise would be to eliminate any possibility of conducting international relations on a moral and rational basis. It is for this reason Farer observes that:

> I have clung for many years to the belief that national decision-makers and the states whose resources they deploy are subjects of international law in a sense qualitatively indistinguishable from Al Capone's subjection to the laws of the state of Illinois and Arab terrorists to the homicide law of West Germany.[4]

The second approach to international law lies at the other end of the spectrum from the "absolutist" view. This theory holds that legal norms in the international system are relatively unimportant. At best international law is only one of several factors to be taken into account when analyzing the behavior of nations.[5] At worst, it is a sham.[6] Obviously, there also would not be a conflict between national security and international law under this scheme. National interests would usually, if not always, prevail.

One person who is sometimes considered to be an advocate of the second approach is Hans J. Morgenthau. He does not dismiss international law as trivial or worthless.[7] But he does believe that in the overall context of international relations it has only a limited role to play. This is because "international law is a primitive type of law resembling the kind of law that prevails in certain preliterate societies, such as the Australian aborigines and the Yurok of northern California."[8] He adds that it is a "primitive type of law primarily because it is almost completely decentralized."[9] Note how Morgenthau characterizes international law in a manner that is in complete opposition to Farer's view. For Farer the normative force of international law is just as strong as that of domestic law. Morgenthau, on the other hand, considers international legal norms to be so primitive and ineffectual as to be inferior to domestic laws in terms of utility.

The decentralized nature of international law means that it is critically dependent upon a community of interest among individual nations and a balance of power between them.[10] Without these two vital assets international law cannot function properly or even at all.[11] The importance of the balance of power prompts Morgenthau to assert that the enforcement of international legal rights ultimately rests upon the ability of a nation to defend itself and upon the "assistance of powerful friends."[12] He observes that "(w)hether such assistance will be forthcoming is a matter not of international law but of national interest as conceived by the individual nations. . . . "[13] In the final analysis, then, international law will often be subservient to the national interest. And the most important interest of any state is the preservation of its security.

The third approach to the nature of international law embodies a compromise between the two extreme positions. It maintains that while international law does not constitute an absolute normative standard, legal norms should be given extreme deference. Put another way, international law should not only be taken into account, it should also be accorded the highest priority during decision-making. This does not mean that a nation cannot or should not violate international law. On rare occasions and for compelling reasons such a decision might be appropriate and necessary. But in the vast majority of cases a state should strictly adhere to the dictates of international law.

This "middle way" has been espoused by many prominent lawyers and analysts including John Norton Moore. With regard to international law he wrote that "it is entitled to great weight from national decision-makers and it ought to control, in almost every context, when in conflict with other considerations."[14] He concludes that "I can think of no recent foreign-policy decision where the illegality of a policy should not have been sufficient alone to bar it."[15]

There are several reasons for preferring the third approach to the other two views. International law to a large extent does codify the past practices and current expectations of the international community as to the legitimate behavior of nation-states.[16] In turn these legal rules and normative principles go far to reduce the potential for chaos in international relations. International law provides policy-makers with useful and fairly well accepted standards with which to judge the behavior of their state and predict the actions of others. With regard to the use of force it is particularly helpful because its norms explicitly seek to limit the frequency and destructiveness of conflicts. Moreover, international law also embodies considerations of fairness, morality, and justice. It does more than merely regulate transnational behavior, it also attempts to provide the international community with at least a semblance of an ethical framework. As such international law offers international relations two valuable commodities: predictability and respectability.

Consequently, it would be improper and very questionable to maintain that international law is merely a sham or just another (trivial) consideration. To down-play or neglect it altogether would be to throw-over six hundred years of accepted wisdom concerning the behavior of nations. Those scholars who suggest that legal norms can be ignored at will or on a frequent basis apparently fail to realize that it is in the long-term interests of states to adhere to international law. To do otherwise would only increase the discord and confusion already inherent in the international system. Although international law may be imperfect, adherence to it is far better than acting solely on the basis of national interest. For all of these reasons the second or deprecatory approach to international law should be dismissed.

Likewise, the "absolutist" view of international law is also flawed. It assumes that all possible contingencies that a nation might face are amenable to regulation by legal principle. Yet it taxes the credulity of decision-makers to suggest that international law has a correct or palatable solution for every problem encountered in the international system. Among other things this view presumes that such important factors as weapons technology, human nature, or standards of morality will always remain constant. In fact, circumstances continually change. As a result it is certainly conceivable that international law might be found to be inadequate to deal with every threat impinging upon a nation's security.

Moore uses an interesting hypothetical example to press home this point. He writes:

> Suppose a particular action were clearly illegal under most interpretations of present law but it were certain that to fail to execute it would result immediately in a full-scale nuclear exchange which could kill more than 200 million people. Should illegality bar the action?[17]

Moore answers "no". Dean Acheson, the former United States Secretary of State and a lawyer, took a similar position when analyzing the Cuban Missile Crisis. He said:

> I must conclude that propriety of the Cuban quarantine is not a legal issue. The power, the position and prestige of the United States had been challenged by another state; and law simply does not deal with such questions of ultimate power. . . . No law can destroy the state creating the law. The survival of states is not a matter of law.[18]

For Moore and Acheson, then, there may be cases where international law will be unable to answer the security needs of individual states. Furthermore, it certainly seems counterintuitive to suggest that a legal norm which results in the destruction of a peaceful nation is also somehow capable of promoting the interests of the international community. After all, one of the most important goals of international law is to prevent the wholesale destruction of nations, cultures, and peoples. Any law that indirectly leads to such a result would actually undermine the very goal it was created to promote. Therefore, it is possible as a theoretical matter that in rare instances states should take action for reasons of national security which would contravene international law. The question remains, however, whether there are any specific instances where such action might be necessary. This issue will be pursued in the following section.

III. NATIONAL SECURITY.

There does seem to be at least one national security circumstance that might on occasion overreach international law. This is the menace posed by the development, deployment or use of nuclear weapons. It is perhaps not surprising that both Moore and Acheson cited instances involving the threat or use of nuclear weapons to highlight the possible limitations of international law. In order to bring this problem into focus it is necessary to examine the nature of nuclear weapons and the current legal norms pertaining to the use of force.

The United Nations Charter is generally considered to be the principal authority for international law on problems relating to the use of force. The two most pertinent sections of the Charter are Articles 2(4) and 51. Article 2(4) proscribes the use of force as an instrument of international relations. It reads in part: "All Members shall refrain in their international relations from the threat or use of force against the territorial integrity or political independence of any state. . . . " Article 51, however, does allow a nation to legally use force for purposes of self-defense. It reads in part: "Nothing in the present Charter shall impair the inherent right of individual or collective self-defense if an armed attack occurs against a Member of the United Nations. . . . " Most authorities construe Article 51 to restrict the legality of forcible self-help to instances involving only self-defense.[19] Other forms of self-help which use force, such as reprisals or humanitarian intervention, are customarily considered to be illegal.[20]

The main problem with Article 51 is that if interpreted literally it would restrict self-defense only to those instances where a nation has actually been attacked. The state would have to wait until an armed assault had actually occurred before it could legally use force to defend itself. With the advent of mechanized warfare this seems to be a fairly high price to pay to stay on the right side of the law. In response to this legitimate criticism most lawyers now concede (although there is still some dispute)[21] that nations may under certain circumstances engage in preemptive or anticipatory self-defense.[22] That is, a defending state may strike the other nation first in order to lessen the blow of the expected attack. This view of Article 51 is certainly supported by state practice since 1945.

The guidelines for anticipatory self-defense, and self-defense in general, spring from customary international law that dates back to at least the nineteenth century. The leading opinion in this area is probably the *Caroline* case.[23] It dealt with events that occurred during an insurrection in Canada in 1837. An American ship, the *Caroline,* was used by rebels to ferry military aid from the United States to Canada. The Canadians responded by entering American territory and destroying the *Caroline.* Several Americans were killed and injured in the attack. The United States protested, declaring that the action was not a proper exercise of the right of self-defense. In order to assess the propriety of the attack Daniel Webster devised a legal test for self-defense. Almost 150 years later the "*Caroline* test" is still considered to be the leading principle on self-defense.[24]

The test consists of two parts, both of which must be met for the act to be legal. Acts of self-defense must be *necessary* and *proportionate*.[25] An act is necessary if it responds to an actual or threatened use of force. If the use of force is only threatened, then the threat must be imminent and "create an instant and over-whelming necessity to respond."[26] Also, the act of self-defense must be exercised only under conditions "leaving no choice of means and no moment for deliberation."[27] In short, all other alternative responses must have been exhausted or have become patently unworkable before force can be used.[28]

The act of self-defense must in addition be proportionate. The response cannot be excessive or unreasonable as compared to the actual or threatened use of force.[29] For example, a nation cannot respond to a limited conventional attack by retaliating with a full-scale thermonuclear strike. This part of the test essentially embodies the ancient principle of "an eye for an eye."

The *Caroline* test is not without its drawbacks, however. The most important part of the test is its allowance for responses against threatened violence. But it is unclear just what exactly constitutes an "imminent" threat or "instant and overwhelming necessity". For most lawyers this would probably be any armed attack which would be likely to occur within a matter of minutes, hours, or at most a few days. Threats of violence that would take weeks, months, or years to blossom into an actual attack probably would not be considered imminent or instant. Thus, under the United Nations Charter and current customary international law an anticipatory attack made against a threatening weapons system which would not become operational for several months or years would be illegal.

This line of legal analysis has very disturbing ramifications when linked to the threat or use of nuclear weapons. This is because nuclear weapons are without question the greatest threat facing individual nations and even the entire international community today. They are the premier weapons of mass destruction.

Nuclear weapons are incredibly destructive. A single one megaton bomb with an explosive power equivalent to 1,000,000 tons of TNT is capable of totally destroying about 200 square miles of territory.[30] In all it would inflict damage across an area of almost 2,000 square miles.[31] The one megaton bomb, like all nuclear weapons, would produce a bright light flash, intense heat, blast and shock waves, an electromagnetic pulse (EMP) of high intensity, radioactive fallout, and possibly severe environmental effects.[32]

The light flash from a one megaton weapon would temporarily blind people looking directly at it from as far away as 100 miles.[33] The heat would vaporize practically everything within three miles of the point of detonation (called ground zero).[34] This would amount to a zone of vaporization of approximately thirty square miles. Many substances up to eight miles from ground zero would spontaneously ignite.[35] This effect would probably cause a firestorm[36], a massive fire that would rage unchecked until all combustible material had been consumed. The blast would create enormous overpressures and strong winds of up to 700 miles an hour.[37] The vast majority of brick houses and buildings would be destroyed within four miles of ground zero.[38] The electromagnetic pulse would disrupt all electromagnetic devices within many miles of the detonation. Radios, televisions, computers, telephones, radars, and power systems would be severely harmed.[39] The nuclear weapon would also produce about 200 radioactive elements in the fallout of dust and particles after the explosion.[40] Many of the radioactive isotopes would exist for thousands of years. The resultant radioactivity would cause radiation sickness and deleterious genetic effects for a period extending from several weeks to several years.[41]

Finally, Carl Sagan and his colleagues calculate that if 1,000 one megaton bombs were detonated almost simultaneously over urban and forested areas, they could cause enough damage to drastically change the weather.[42] The smoke, dust, and debris caused by the explosions and resultant fires would rise into the atmosphere and block out the sunlight. As a result surface land temperatures could fall to minus four degrees Fahrenheit. Temperatures would stay below the freezing point of water for up to seventy days after the detonations.[43] Therefore, even a limited nuclear war would create a man-made "nuclear winter". In this regard it is interesting to note that the United States and the Soviet Union together possess over 42,000 nuclear weapons of various sizes.[44] If a large proportion of them were used the environmental effects would be even worse. A nuclear conflict using 10,000 megatons would cause surface land temperatures to fall to minus twenty degrees Fahrenheit. The temperature would remain below freezing for well over five months.[45]

Sagan predicts that the reduction in temperatures would not be confined to the areas attacked by nuclear weapons. The worldwide weather patterns would spread the atmospheric debris across every hemisphere. The environmental effects of a nuclear attack would thus be global.[46] Furthermore, Paul Ehrlich and his coworkers predict that a severe enough nuclear winter (5,000 to 10,000 megaton exchange) could destroy most of the large life forms inhabiting the surface of the earth.[47] This means that the human race could be largely destroyed or actually become extinct. Certainly the environmental effects would destroy the international system as we now know it.

The destructiveness of nuclear weapons is further increased by rapid advances in delivery system technology and component miniaturization. Nuclear weapons can be delivered with excellent accuracy by intercontinental ballistic missiles (ICBMs), sea-launched ballistic missiles (SLBMs), most military aircraft, many different types of cruise missiles, short-and-medium range ballistic missiles, and even artillery shells. ICBMs, for example, are capable of carrying several large nuclear warheads over 8,000 miles in less than thirty minutes.[48] Each warhead would land less than 250 yards from its intended target. Even short-range rockets like the United States Army's Lance missile can carry a nuclear warhead up to seventy-six miles at over 2,200 miles an hour.[49] This means that a defender would have at most only about two minutes of warning to respond to the attack.

The miniaturization of nuclear weapons is also a major problem. Relatively crude bombs can be built to fit into large cars or small trucks.[50] The vehicles could be dispersed in various locations within the defending country. All of the bombs could then be detonated simultaneously, giving the defender absolutely no warning of an impending strike.

Nations with limited infrastructures or small geographical sizes are particularly threatened by nuclear weapons. Israel, for instance, has an area of only about 12,000 square miles (including the occupied territories).[51] Since a one megaton bomb can inflict damage over an area of 2,000 square miles, it would only take five such bombs to ruin almost the entire state of Israel. On the other hand, although Australia is a very large nation geographically, it has a limited infrastructure. Sixty-five percent[52] of its population resides in five cities.* This means that five one megaton weapons would be enough to kill or injure almost two-thirds of Australia's fifteen million inhabitants.

To compound this threat more and more nations are acquiring the necessary technology to construct and deliver nuclear weapons. At present the United States, Soviet Union, Great Britain, France, and the Peoples Republic of China possess nuclear weapons. In all probability Israel also has the bomb.[53] And India, at least, has detonated a "nuclear device". Approximately fourteen** other nations have the capability to manufacture a bomb within a minimum of three years.[54] Potential members of the nuclear club include Argentina, Pakistan, South Africa, and Taiwan.

The proliferation problem is particularly worrisome because it substantially increases the probability that nuclear weapons will

---

*Sydney (3,474,000), Melbourne (2,994,600), Brisbane (1,101,700), Adelaide (1,035,000), and Perth (925,700) have an aggregate population of more than 9,500,000.

**The fourteen are: Argentina, Australia, Canada, Italy, Japan, Mexico, Pakistan, South Africa, Spain, Sweden, Switzerland, Taiwan, West Germany, and Yugoslavia.

someday be used.[55] A greater number of bombs worldwide increases the likelihood of an accidental detonation, loss or even theft of a nuclear weapon. The more nations that possess bombs, the greater the probability that at least one country will find itself in a conflict and perceive the need to use a bomb. And the more often nuclear weapons are placed into the hands of different decision-makers, the more likely it is that they will eventually come under the control of an irrational or unbalanced leader. It is horrible to consider what a man like the Ayatollah Khomeini might do with even one small nuclear weapon.

In sum, nuclear weapons represent a significant threat to the survival of nations. A mere handful of them can totally destroy an entire country. If used in large quantities they can jeopardize the existence of the human race. Therefore, individual nations and the international community should be able to take whatever reasonable precautions are necessary, including the use of force, to prevent the employment of nuclear weapons.

The problem is that international law substantially limits the precautions a state can use to protect itself. In the nuclear world a legal norm such as Article 2(4), which forces a nation to wait for an attack before it can legally use force in response, in effect automatically guarantees the certain destruction of the defender. It is true that the *Caroline* test as applied to Article 51 does allow states to exercise a right of anticipatory self-defense. The drawback is that the threat must be actual and imminent. Thus, a nation which merely possessed nuclear weapons, but did not use them to threaten another nation, would not present an imminent threat to that other nation. Without some actual provocation the defending state would be prohibited from using force to destroy the nuclear weapons of the other state.

This places the defending country in a terrible quandry. In order to protect itself in accordance with the prescribed legal norms it must accomplish two difficult tasks. First, the nation must wait for definite signs of an imminent attack. However, given the current status of delivery technology the nation may not receive any warning at all or at best only a few minutes or hours notice. Second, acting on very short notice the defender must then launch an anticipatory attack that has to be completely successful. Nuclear weapons are so destructive it does not do much good to intercept most of them before they reach their targets. A successful defensive action requires that virtually every attacking warhead be eliminated. If even one gets through it could cause the loss of hundreds of thousands of people. Obviously, under these restrictive conditions even the most competent military establishment would find it extremely difficult to guarantee the survival of its state.

There is further support for the proposition that the Charter and customary international law do not adequately deal with the threat of nuclear weapons. Both the Charter and customary law pre-date the development of nuclear weapons. The *Caroline* test as we saw was devised in the early 1800s. The Charter of the United Nations was signed on June 26, 1945 in San Francisco. At that time the atomic bomb was still a United States military secret. It was not used on Hiroshima until August 6, 1945.

One of the first people to recognize this problem was John Foster Dulles, a former United States Secretary of State and a renowned international lawyer. Dulles took part in the convention at San Francisco that drafted the Charter. Speaking before the American Bar Association in 1953 he said:[56]

> The United Nations Charter now reflects serious inadequacies. One inadequacy sprang from ignorance. When we were in San Francisco in the Spring of 1945, none of us knew of the atomic bomb... The Charter is thus a pre-atomic age charter. In this sense it was obsolete before it actually came into force. As one who was at San Francisco, I can say with confidence that if the delegates there had known that the mysterious and immeasurable power of the atom would be available as a means of mass destruction, the provisions of the Charter dealing with disarmament and the regulation of armaments would have been far more emphatic and realistic.

Given the inadequacies currently prevailing in international law states can adopt several different strategies. One approach is for a nation to find (in the words of Morgenthau) "powerful friends" who already possess nuclear weapons. The hope is that the friend's nuclear weapons will deter an attack by another nuclear power. This is obviously the strategy that Japan and West Germany have adopted. The drawback to this approach is that times change and so do one's friends. History shows that nations who rely on other states for their security have rather modest longevities.

Another policy is to build and deploy one's own nuclear weapons. This deterent strategy works well only if the nation has the scientific, economic, and military infrastructure necessary to construct them. For practical reasons this is an option that is not available to most nations. Also, once the state obtains nuclear weapons it must be able to deploy them in such a way that they will not be destroyed in a surprise or preemptive attack. Otherwise the weapons will not constitute a credible deterrent. Very small states such as Israel suffer from this drawback. A third difficulty with this option is that it will, over the long term, intensify the proliferation problem. As noted previously, as more nations perceive the need to possess nuclear weapons for self-defense the more likely it will be that they will eventually be used.

A third approach is simply to declare that, as a matter of international law, the mere existence of nuclear weapons by definition constitutes an imminent threat, regardless of whether or not they are used provocatively. Under this scheme a nation would be able to exercise a legal right to anticipatory self-defense whenever it felt threatened by another nation's nuclear weapons capability. The problem with this plan is that it creates a loophole in the legal norms pertaining to the use of force large enough to drive a truck through.

A fourth solution is to adopt a principled policy of anticipatory self-defense. In this case a nation would only act after a rigorous set of preconditions had been met. The approach would work only if an objectively meaningful test could be devised that would inform decision-makers when an "unorthodox" national security action might be advisable. Such a test will be outlined in the next section.

IV. PROPOSED FRAMEWORK.

Several scholars have devised tests and analytical criteria to assess the propriety of a state's use of force. Two of the most successful efforts were made by Richard A. Falk and James J. McHugh. Falk proposed a legal framework using twelve criteria to analyze the use of force in retaliation against prior terroristic acts in times of peace.[57] By modifying Falk's criteria McHugh developed a test to determine when the use of force by states is "reasonable" and "tolerable".[58] McHugh explicitly considers his "Falk's modified criteria" to be applicable to all instances of forcible self-help including self-defense, intervention, and retaliation.[59] In this respect his test has a wider application than Falk's original criteria. However, neither scholar specifically addressed the problems associated with the threat of nuclear weapons.

McHugh's criteria are given below:[60]

> The use of force by states may be acceptable provided:
> - That acts of provocation by the target state have raised an imminent and significant threat to the continued existence of a nation's political independence and/or territorial integrity.
> - That, if possible, a diligent effort has been made to obtain satisfaction by pacific means.
> - That recourse to international organizations is had as practicable.
> - That a state accepts the burden of persuasion and makes a prompt explanation of its conduct before the relevant organ of community review, showing a disposition to accord respect to its will.
> - That the acting state's purpose cannot be achieved by acting within its own territory.
> - That the use of force is proportional to the provocation and directed against military and paramilitary targets and clearly indicates the contours of the unacceptable provocation.
> - That the user of force continues to seek a pacific settlement of the underlying dispute on reasonable terms.

Although the criteria represent an excellent framework for analyzing the use of force in general, they do present a few problems when dealing specifically with nuclear weapons. There are two difficulties with the first criterion. First, the defending state can only respond to "acts of provocation". It is unclear exactly what this means, but it probably implies some sort of actual attack or threatened violence. The problem, of course, is that the mere development or possession of nuclear weapons would not ordinarily constitute a "provocative" act in the strictest sense of the word. Yet even the possession of a nuclear weapons capability can be extremely threatening. Second, McHugh explicitly maintains that the threat responded to must be "imminent".[61] This is a significant drawback. As we have seen, forcing a state to wait until a nuclear weapons threat becomes imminent or instant could result in the total destruction of the defender even if it were able to conduct an anticipatory attack. In order to be effective against a nuclear threat states often would have to act long before the threat became "imminent" in the normally accepted meaning of the term.

Another problem concerns the sixth criterion. McHugh suggests that force should only be directed against military and "paramilitary" targets. The difficulty is that nuclear weapons facilities often include scientific research laboratories and nuclear power plants. Any attack on such establishments would undoubtedly endanger individuals who were clearly civilians or non-governmental workers. It is unclear whether a paramilitary target under Falk's and McHugh's usage would incorporate such facilities and personnel. Their use of the term paramilitary probably meant to embrace terroristic organizations such as the PLO and the Red Brigades.[62]

With these objections in mind the criteria can be rearranged to construct an analytical framework which can accomodate the special properties of nuclear weapons. It must be emphasized that the test developed here is meant only to cover acts of anticipatory self-defense made in response to a nuclear weapons threat. It is not intended to be a general framework for evaluating all forms of forcible self-help. However, the term "nuclear weapons threat" is used in the broadest context. It is meant to include the acquisition of a nuclear weapons technology as well as the production of actual weapons. It also includes the deployment of nuclear weapons and their threatened and actual use. The objective of the framework is to provide policymakers with a set of criteria that would allow them to make a realistic yet principled decision about a possible use of force against a nuclear weapons threat.

A summary of the proposed test is given below:

1. The nuclear weapons threat must constitute a radical and significant threat to the responding nation's territorial integrity or political independence.
2. The response to the nuclear weapons threat must be an action of last resort.
3. The response must be proportionate to the level of the nuclear weapons threat.
4. The responding nation must accept the burden of persuasion for its action.

5. The overall response, including the application of force, must be calculated to avoid a repetition of the nuclear weapons threat.

In order for the proposed national security action to be considered "legitimate" or principled all five criteria must be satisfied by a preponderance of the evidence. A closer examination of each criterion will show how this might be accomplished.

The first criterion requires that the threat must be radical and significant. Clearly nuclear weapons *per se* strongly threaten any nation's territorial integrity and political independence. In this sense the threat is significant. But the threat must also be radically new or different in nature. It must profoundly disturb the status quo. There are three different ways a nation can create a "radical" nuclear weapons threat. First, it could acquire a genuine technological capability to construct a nuclear bomb. A state's transformation from a non-nuclear power into a nuclear weapons power would be an event that could be classified as a radical change. Second, a nation could already possess nuclear weapons but elect to deploy them in a provocative or threatening manner. For example, the weapons could be deployed in such a way as to drastically reduce the time it would take to conduct a surprise first-strike. Third, the nation could deploy a new type of nuclear weapons system that would rapidly and significantly alter the balance of power or correlation of forces.

A radical threat is certainly not meant to include incremental changes in the size, deployment or technological capability of nuclear forces already possessed by states. For instance, since the Soviet Union already possesses several thousand nuclear weapons and hundreds of delivery vehicles, the deployment of an additional 100 SS-18 "heavy" ICBMs would not represent a radical threat to the United States. Also, and perhaps this goes without saying, a significant threat would occur only if the responding state had definite reason to believe that nuclear weapons might at some point be used against it. A nation could not attack a state possessing nuclear weapons simply on the off chance that they might be used against the responding state at a later date. In this respect the threat must be actual if not necessarily imminent. Factors that would indicate an actual threat include the rationality and bellicosity of the nuclear weapons state's leadership and the degree of past and present hostility between the two nations.

The second criterion is meant to incorporate the "necessity" part of the *Caroline* test. The exercise of anticipatory self-defense must be an act of last resort. All other means to resolve the nuclear weapons threat must have been exhausted or shown to be patently unlikely to succeed if attempted. This includes recourse to international organizations, in particular the United Nations Security Council and the International Atomic Energy Agency (IAEA). In short, the use of force must be a calculated act of desperation after all pacific attempts have failed.

The third criterion is meant to embrace the "proportionality" aspect of the *Caroline* test. The response must be directed specifically against the nuclear weapons threat. This does not mean that the response cannot be thorough. Legitimate targets could include nuclear weapons research, production, and storage facilities as well as specialized delivery vehicles. Targets could also include ostensible civilian installations if they were directly associated with nuclear weapons. Three rigorous guidelines would have to be met, however. First, any response would have to keep casualties and loss of life for every party to the action down to a bare minimum. Second, the response must be designed to reduce significantly any possibility of radioactive contamination by the destruction of fissile materials at the target. Third, a state must *never* use nuclear weapons to eliminate a nuclear weapons threat. Any such response would be by definition an unproportionate and unprincipled use of force. If nuclear weapons were allowed to be used then the primary goal of preventing their use would obviously be subverted. Only conventional force may be used.

The fourth criterion closely corresponds to McHugh's fourth principle. The responding state must accept the burden of persuasion for its action. Specifically, it must immediately and fully explain the reason for its act to the target state and the international community. The responding state must also accept the burden for its conduct in another respect. It should compensate innocent third parties for any harm they may have incurred as a result of the act. For example, an action might release radioactive debris into a nearby third country. The responding nation should indemnify the third country for the cost of cleaning-up the radioactive contamination.

The fifth criterion is unquestionably the most important one.

The use of force against a nuclear weapons technology is pointless and counterproductive if it only serves to create a similar or worse threat at a later time. The response must be calculated to avoid a repetition of the threat. This could be accomplished in one of three ways. First, the threat could be permanently eliminated by the use of force. Second, the threat could be temporarily alleviated by the application of force. Subsequently the responding state could use pacific means such as negotiation to resolve the underlying problem. Third, the threat could be temporarily moderated. The responding state could then use the additional time gained to take other military and political measures to reduce its susceptibility to future nuclear threats.

Another way to phrase the fifth criterion might be to say that the response must be calculated to avoid the use of nuclear weapons. This principle explicitly incorporates the primary assumption underlying the entire analytical framework. The assumption is that a nuclear war should be avoided at practically all costs. This means that the use of conventional force should be considered to be principled, or at least tolerable, if it will directly lead to a reduction in the possibility of a nuclear conflict.

Now many scholars might object to the test presented here because it encourages the use of force. As such it promotes military conflict and political instability. They might add that this view explicitly contradicts the prohibitions against the use of force embodied in the United Nations Charter. To a certain extent this criticism is correct. The criteria do promote acts of forcible self-help, but with the critical caveat that they must take place only under very specialized and limited circumstances. Once again it must be emphasized that the potential use of nuclear weapons must be reduced as much as possible. If this can be done by precise applications of conventional force under strict conditions, then it would be a distasteful but worthwhile price to pay. In the final analysis a few limited conventional conflicts would seem to be far preferable to the detonation of even one nuclear weapon over an urban target.

V. APPLICATION OF THE FRAMEWORK.

It might be instructive to apply the proposed framework to an actual case. There have been a number of situations in the past where nations have forcefully responded to a nuclear weapons threat. There will undoubtedly be more such instances in the future.

One classic example was the Cuban Missile Crisis of 1962. In that situation the United States carefully threatened a limited use of force in the form of a naval blockade (euphemistically called a "quarantine"). The objective was to compel the Soviet Union to withdraw its intermediate-range nuclear missiles from Cuba. The Soviets eventually complied with the American request and the United States for its part never did actually use any force. The Soviets have continued to refrain from placing nuclear offensive weapons back into Cuba. In this sense the missile quarantine seems to have satisfied the fifth criterion. Although the American action was somewhat questionable under international law,[63] many if not most non-Communist analysts would probably say that it was a valid and successful effort to deal with a nuclear weapons threat.

Another more recent example is the Israeli airstrike against Iraq's nuclear reactor complex on June 7, 1981. The raid was undertaken in order to slow down or prevent Iraq from acquiring a nuclear weapons capability. The Israelis were convinced that the facility would enable Iraq to produce nuclear weapons.[64] They also strongly believed that Iraq would not hesitate to use them against Israel.[65]

The Israelis dispatched fourteen fighter-bomber aircraft to attack the nuclear installation.[66] The facility is located in the town of Tuwaitha near Baghdad. The aircraft dropped sixteen 2,000 pound conventional bombs on or near the Osirak* nuclear reactor.[67] The reactor, the sole target of the attack, was destroyed.[68] The Israelis also inadvertently killed three Iraqi civilians and one French engineer working on the project.[69] The airstrike lasted about two minutes.[70] At the time of the attack the reactor had not been "loaded" with radioactive fuel. It was therefore not yet operational.[71]

There were several questionable aspects about Iraq's nuclear program in general and the Osirak reactor in particular. First, the Osirak reactor was a seventy megawatt materials testing reactor

---

*The French, who supplied the reactor to the Iraqis, refer to it as the Osirak. The Iraqis renamed the reactor the Tammuz I.

that did not have a capability to produce electric power. It could not be used for an indigenous power program.[72] Instead it was an extremely large and powerful scientific research device. Although the Iraqis could legitimately use a research reactor, the Osirak-type seemed far too sophisticated for their fledgling nuclear science program.[73]

Second, the Iraqis insisted that the French provide ninety-three percent enriched uranium to fuel the reactor. This was a significant demand because uranium enriched to that degree can easily be used to construct nuclear weapons. Bowing to Iraqi pressure, the French agreed to provide about seventy kilograms of the weapons-grade fuel. Later, however, they attempted to persuade Iraq to use a less enriched type of uranium that could not be used to make nuclear weapons. The Iraqis adamantly refused.[74]

Third, before obtaining Osirak from France the Iraqis attempted to purchase a gas-graphite reactor that was specially designed to produce plutonium. Plutonium is an even better fissionable material for making nuclear weapons than enriched uranium. The French refused to sell the gas-graphite reactor.[75]

Fourth, Iraq acquired from Italy a "hot-cell" device that could be used to extract and refine plutonium from radioactive wastes and depleted reactor fuels.[76]

Fifth, Iraq purchased 250 tons of natural uranium. The uranium could have been placed around the fuel rods of the Osirak reactor to produce about five to ten kilograms of plutonium a year.[77] The Iraqis then could have used their "hot-cells" to extract the plutonium. The purchase of such a large quantity of natural uranium was especially interesting because not one of Iraq's reactors could use it as a fuel.[78]

Finally, it was unclear just exactly why Iraq wanted to create such a large nuclear research establishment. The nation had more than enough oil to supply its power and industrial needs. Also, it was only after the 1973 October War, in which Israel decisively defeated Iraq, that the Iraqis began to place greater emphasis on their nuclear program.[79]

Given the intense and long-standing enmity between the two countries, the Israelis viewed these developments with great alarm. They concluded that the Iraqis were deliberately acquiring the technology and infrastructure necessary to produce nuclear weapons materials. It seemed to be only a matter of time before Iraq built an atomic bomb. Accordingly the Israelis asserted that their airstrike was a legal act of anticipatory self-defense under both the United Nations Charter and customary international law.[80] In reality, however, the raid was a clear violation of international law.

The problem concerns the exact nature of the Iraqi threat. Under the *Caroline* test, of course, a threat must be instant. Iraq's ability to *use* nuclear weapons would therefore have to be imminent. Yet practically all authorities believe that it would have taken Iraq several years at the time of the attack to construct even one bomb.[81] For example, Roger Richter, a former official of the International Atomic Energy Agency (IAEA), testified before Congress that it would have been years in the future before Iraq could have developed a nuclear weapon.[82] Christopher Chant and Ian Hogg, authors of *Nuclear War in the 1980s,* estimate that it would have taken a minimum of six to ten years.[83] Finally, the prestigious International Institute for Strategic Studies (IISS) stated:

> Thus by June 1981, when a flight of Israeli F-16s, escorted by a number of F-15s, dropped roughly 30 tons of bombs and destroyed the Osirak reactor building, it had become clear that Iraq was indeed interested in developing a modern nuclear technology. There were even several signs indicating her interest in a nuclear weapons option. *But none of the signs suggested that the Iraqi programme was very close to realizing this option, and it was estimated that another four to six years would be needed for this.*[84] (Emphasis added.)

This timing problem makes it impossible to classify the Iraqi threat as imminent. By no stretch of the imagination can a time lapse of several years be construed as an event "about to occur". Therefore, Israel cannot justify its use of force under the *Caroline* test and international law.

Nonetheless, the airstrike might have been a principled use of force under our five "national security and nuclear weapons criteria". Recall that the first criterion requires that the nuclear weapons threat must be radical and significant. Since the Iraqis apparently were acquiring nuclear weapons technology, it would seem that they were attempting to disturb profoundly the status quo. Israel's case is damaged, however, when the significance of the threat is closely analyzed.

It is not at all clear the Iraqis would have been able to use their newly acquired technology to actually make an atomic bomb. Iraq ratified the Non-Proliferation Treaty (NPT) on October 29, 1969. As such it was fully subject to the system of safeguards developed by the IAEA. The safeguards are meant to ensure that the nuclear materials used by a non-nuclear weapons state are not used to construct nuclear weapons. From the very beginning Iraq opened her nuclear installations, including the Osirak reactor, to inspection by the IAEA.[85]

Now there are two ways Iraq could have avoided the safeguards in order to obtain the necessary nuclear materials. First, it could have "diverted" some of the enriched uranium used to fuel Osirak in order to build a bomb.[86] This would have required the theft of several kilograms. The IAEA Director-General, Sigvard Eklund, stated before the United Nations Security Council on June 12, 1981 that the "design of the [Osirak] facility and of the fuel elements is such that [they] provide assurance that diversion of fuel elements would be detected with a very high probability".[87]

The second method of diversion would have been to produce plutonium clandestinely.[88] The only way to realistically do this would have been to surround the core of the Osirak reactor with a "blanket" of natural uranium.[89] Eklund said that the "size and location of this blanket would be such that ordinary visual inspection would reveal its presence."[90] He concluded that "in a reactor of this type, diversion of fuel elements or of undeclared plutonium produced at low rates cannot be technically excluded, but would be detected with very high probability."[91]

Thus, the Iraqis could have built a bomb only if they had either managed to violate the safeguards over a long period of time or elected to withdraw officially from the IAEA safeguard system. Since it seems very unlikely they would have been able to cheat successfully, the Iraqis would have been forced to quit the IAEA. But it would have been only at this point that they could have actually embarked upon a nuclear weapons program. And it still would have taken them several months or years after leaving the IAEA to collect the necessary nuclear materials and construct a bomb. The Israelis would have had plenty of warning.

There are several other factors which reduce the significance of Iraq's nuclear weapons program. First, at the time of the attack Osirak had not yet become operational. The Iraqis were in absolutely no position to divert materials much less construct a nuclear weapon. Second, a nuclear weapons program requires well trained personnel. Chant and Hogg estimate that the training of Iraq's scientists and technicians was "poor".[92] Third, even if Iraq did divert materials and build a bomb, she would still have to deliver it against Israel. Yet Iraq does not possess any missiles capable of this task.[93] Nor does it have many aircraft with sufficient range and penetration ability.[94] Israel, on the other hand, has a well developed anti-aircraft system and the latest American interceptor aircraft.[95]

For all these reasons Iraq's nuclear weapons program had not yet become a significant threat. The Israelis, therefore, acted prematurely. This does not mean they had to wait until a nuclear attack by Iraq was imminent. But they should have at least delayed their attack until Iraq began to divert nuclear materials or construct a bomb. Indications of such activity would include Iraq's withdrawal from the IAEA or evidence that it was violating the safeguard system.

The Israelis also ran afoul of the second criterion. Israel failed to explore fully peaceful means for resolving the threat. The airstrike was not the only option available. Apparently Israel did not attempt any negotiation with Iraq.[96] The problem was not brought up before the Security Council.[97] Nor did she try to work with the IAEA. In fact, to this day, Israel has refused to sign the NPT. She has also refused to submit any part of her own large nuclear establishment to inspection by any foreign representatives including those from the IAEA and the United States.[98] Among other things this means that Israel could not agree to additional IAEA inspections in order to compel Iraq to do likewise.[99] Furthermore, the Israelis refused to accept frequent French protestations that the Osirak program was intended solely for peaceful purposes.[100] Finally, Israel did not involve either superpower in the dispute.[101] The record thus seems to indicate that Israel generally acted alone or at odds with the rest of the international community. In particular, and unlike Iraq, she failed to cooperate with the pertinent international organizations.

Israel did satisfy the third criterion. By any standard the attack would have to be classified as a proportionate use of force. It was a brief and precise airstrike against a single installation directly related to the threat. Only sixteen bombs were used. This is a minimal amount of force. Although there were a total of four fatalities the Israelis clearly meant to keep casualties to a minimum. This is shown by their decision to strike on a Sunday evening, a time when the vast majority of workers were at home.[102]

The fourth criterion was also probably met. The day after the attack the Israelis distributed a release describing the attack and the reasons for it. They also participated fully and forthrightly in the United Nations debates that followed soon after the attack.[103] In short, they did bear the burden of persuasion for their use of force.

The fifth criterion is more troublesome for the Israeli case. It is unclear whether over the long-term the airstrike actually eliminated or contained the nuclear weapons threat posed by Iraq and other Arab states. France agreed immediately after the attack to rebuild the Osirak reactor.[104] However, it did take the opportunity to insist on more stringent safeguards.[105] The French also elected to supply only low-enriched, non-weapons grade uranium to the reactor in the future.[106] The airstrike itself set back Iraq's nuclear program by about three or four years.[107] These developments probably do mean that the attack did stop the nuclear proliferation problem in the Middle East over the short-term.[108] This in turn gives Israel additional time to devise alternate measures to deal with a resumption of the Iraqi threat or the development of another nuclear weapons program elsewhere in the region.[109]

Moreover, although practically every country condemned the raid, the most important actors in the Middle East responded fairly moderately. The airstrike did not jeopardize or severely worsen Israel's relations with either the United States or Egypt.[110] Apparently the Saudi Arabians, including King Khaled, privately expressed satisfaction with the temporary demise of Iraq's nuclear project.[111] The simple truth is no one wanted Iraq to get the bomb. Thus, there are indications that the airstrike might avoid a repetition of the threat over the mid-and-long-term. In any event the airstrike will certainly act as a great deterrent to Iraq and other Arab nations.

On the other hand, the attack did humiliate Iraq in particular and the Arab world in general. It also served to reinforce blatantly Israel's regional monopoly on nuclear weapons. The Arabs must surely find this situation to be intolerable. Therefore, it cannot be said with any degree of certainty that the Arabs will not in the future attempt to acquire nuclear weapons technology. Perhaps the best that can be said is this: over the short-term the airstrike probably was successful, but the outlook for the long-term remains at present shrouded in doubt and fear.

In summary, the application of the five criteria to Israel's use of force against Iraq's nuclear reactor has produced mixed results. Israel clearly failed to satisfy the first two criteria. The nuclear weapons threat was not significant enough to warrant an exercise of forcible self-help. Also, the Israelis did not properly pursue pacific means to settle the problem. Conversely, they did satisfactorily meet the third and fourth criteria. The attack was proportionate and the Israelis did bear the burden of persuasion. As far as the fifth criterion is concerned, it is unclear whether the act was ultimately calculated to avoid a repetition of the threat. In this regard it is important to note that in order for a criterion to be satisfied there must be a preponderance of evidence supporting the national security action. Since this was not the case for the fifth criterion Israel technically did not satisfy it as well. Overall, then, Israel failed to meet three of the five criteria. Recall that *all* five criteria must be satisfied for the action to be considered principled. Therefore, the Israeli airstrike was not only a violation of international law, it was also an unprincipled and illegitimate use of force.

VI. NATURE OF THE TEST.

One final issue remains to be discussed. This concerns the precise nature of the test presented here. The proposed framework is not meant to codify or represent existing international law. Although it does incorporate many current legal norms, the test does not necessarily differentiate between imminent and non-imminent nuclear weapons threats as long as they are radical and significant. Under some circumstances then the criteria might offend the *Caroline* test and present international law.

Furthermore, the test is not meant to extend or change the current contours of international law. It is not being suggested here that the law has implicitly evolved, or that it should be amended, to conform to the five criteria.

Rather the test was devised with the knowledge that it might endorse national security actions that would violate international law. Now it might seem bizarre and paradoxical to advocate that states should break the law under some circumstances, but only in a principled manner. By definition law breaking appears to be illegitimate and unprincipled. There are two reasons why this seemingly contradictory course was adopted.

First, there is the reality of the behavior of nations. As Dean Acheson observed, nations will not obey the law when their self-preservation is at stake. Nothing threatens the existence of states more than the use of nuclear weapons. The problems associated with their development and use may be a realm where jurisprudential norms just do not operate satisfactorily. This does not mean, however, that nations should act nefariously or irrationally. The test is meant to help fill this normative void.

Second, the test is intended to be a compromise between two competing interests. The threat of nuclear conflict must be reduced. Yet the use of force as an instrument of international relations must also be condemned and avoided. One way to satisfy these two goals is to say that nations can act somewhat ruthlessly to prevent nuclear war, but they must also pay a price for their ruthless behavior. They must operate outside of the law. They must act at their own risk without the benefit of the international legal system. This in turn should help deter the use of force except in situations of extreme necessity.

Moreover, if the proposed test were to be incorporated into international law it would in effect create an exception for the use of force on the basis of nuclear weapons and self-preservation. This would probably create a large loophole in the norms pertaining to forcible self-help. Nations would begin to justify all of their actions on the basis of self-preservation. Alternatively, they would concoct the flimsiest of connections between their use of force and nuclear weapons threats in order to call their actions legal. The result might be an increase in the use of force without a corresponding decrease in the potential for nuclear conflict. This would make an absolute mockery of international law.

For these reasons the proposed test is meant to provide principled guidance for decision-makers without asserting that every action they might undertake would be legal. Perhaps in this way nuclear war might be avoided without an excessive cost in terms of either the use of force or damage to international law.

NOTES

1. *See* Article 1 of the Convention on International Civil Aviation (The Chicago Convention) of December 7, 1944, 61 Stat. 1180, 15 U.N.T.S. 295.
2. Tom J. Farer, "On Professor Moore's Synthesis," in John Norton Moore (ed.), *Law and Civil War in the Modern World* (Baltimore: Johns Hopkins University Press, 1974), p. 564.
3. *Ibid.*
4. *Ibid.,* p. 564.
5. Hans J. Morgenthau, *The Politics of Nations: The Struggle for Power and Peace* (Fifth Edition, Revised) (New York: Alfred A. Knopf, 1978), p. 279.
6. *Ibid.*
7. *Ibid.*, pp. 280–281.
8. *Ibid.,* p. 281.
9. *Ibid.*
10. *Ibid.,* p. 282.
11. *Ibid.,* p. 298.
12. *Ibid.*
13. *Ibid.*
14. John Norton Moore, "On Professor Farer's Need for a Thesis: A Reply," in John Norton Moore (ed.) *Law and Civil War in the Modern World* (Baltimore: Johns Hopkins University Press, 1974), p. 571.
15. *Ibid.*
16. *Ibid.*
17. *Ibid.*
18. Remarks by the Honorable Dean Acheson, American Society of International Law, *Proceedings of the American Society of International Law at Its Fifty-Seventh Annual Meeting* (Washington: 1963), p. 14.
19. James J. McHugh, "Forcible Self-Help in International Law," 62 *United States Naval War College International Legal Studies* 87 (1980), p. 96.
20. *Ibid.,* p. 98.
21. *See, for example,* M. Nagendra Singh, "The Right of Self-Defense in Relation to the Use of Nuclear Weapons," 5 *Indian Year Book of International Affairs* 3 (1956), p. 24.
22. McHugh, *op. cit.,* p. 91.
23. *Ibid.*
24. *Ibid.*

25. *Ibid.*
26. *Ibid.*
27. *Ibid.*
28. *Ibid.*
29. *Ibid.*
29. *Ibid.*
30. R. P. Turco, O. B Toon, T. P. Ackerman, J. B Pollock, and Carl Sagan, "Nuclear Winter: Global Consequences of Multiple Nuclear Explosions," 222 *Science* 1283 (23 December 1983), p. 1284. Hereinafter cited as "Sagan".
31. Christopher Chant and Ian Hogg, *Nuclear War in the 1980's* (New York: Nomad Publishers Ltd., 1983). pp. 138–139.
32. *Ibid.*
33. *Ibid.*
34. *Ibid.*
35. *Ibid.*
36. *Ibid.*
37. *Ibid.*
38. *Ibid.*
39. *Ibid.*
40. *Ibid.*
41. *Ibid.*
42. Sagan, *op. cit.,* p. 1283.
43. *Ibid.,* p. 1287.
44. Stockholm International Peace Research Institute, *The Arms Race and Arms Control 1983* (New York: Taylor & Francis, Inc., 1983), p. 27.
45. Sagan, *op. cit.,* p. 1283.
46. *Ibid.*
47. Paul R. Ehrlich *et. al.,* "Long-Term Biological Consequences of Nuclear War," 222 *Science* 1293 (23 December 1983), p. 1293.
48. Chant and Hogg, *op. cit.,* p. 84.
49. *Ibid.,* p. 108.
50. *Ibid.,* p. 66.
51. *The World Almanac & Book of Facts 1982* (New York: Newspaper Enterprise Association, Inc., 1982), p. 549.
52. *Ibid.,* pp. 516–517.
53. Chant and Hogg, *op. cit.,* p. 59.
54. *Ibid.*
55. Lewis A. Dunn, *Controlling the Bomb: Nuclear Proliferation if the 1980s* (New Haven: Yale University Press. 1982), pp. 69–71.
56. Address by the Honorable John Foster Dulles, Secretary of State, Before the American Bar Association, Boston, Mass., August 26,

1953, at 2:30 PM E.S.T., State Department Release Number 458, p. 6.
57. Richard A. Falk, "The Beirut Raid and the International Law of Retaliation," 63 *Am. J. Int'l L.* 415 (1969), pp. 438–442.
58. McHugh, *op. cit.,* p. 101.
59. *Ibid.*
60. *Ibid.,* p. 102.
61. *Ibid.*
62. Falk, *op. cit.,* p. 441.
63. Myres McDougal, "The Soviet-Cuban Quarantine and Self-Defense," 57 *Am. J. Int'l L.* 597 (1963).
64. Shai Feldman, "The Bombing of Osirak—Revisted," 7 *International Security* 114 (1982), p. 122.
65. *Ibid.*
66. Joanne Birnberg, "The Sun Sets on Tammuz I: The Israeli Raid on Iraq's Nuclear Reactor, 13 *Ca. W. Int'l L. J.* 86 (1983), p. 86.
67. *Ibid.*
68. *Ibid.*
69. Thomas Mallison and Sally Mallison, "The Israeli Aerial Attack of June 7, 1981: Aggression or Self-Defense?," 15 *Vanderbilt J. Transnat'l L.* 417 (1982), p. 418.
70. Birnberg, *op. cit.,* p. 86.
71. *Ibid.*
72. Feldman, *op. cit.,* p. 115.
73. *Ibid.,* p. 116.
74. *Ibid.,* pp. 116–117.
75. *Ibid.,* p. 115.
76. *Ibid.,* p. 118.
77. *Ibid.,* p. 116.
78. *Ibid.,* pp. 117–118.
79. International Institute for Strategic Studies, *Strategic Survey 1981–1982* (London: IISS, 1982), p. 19. Hereinafter cited as "IISS".
80. Mallison and Mallison, *op. cit.,* p. 418.
81. *Ibid.*
82. The Israeli Air Strike: Hearings Before the Senate Foreign Relations Committee, 97th Cong., 1st Sess., 1981, p. 108.
83. Chant and Hogg, *op. cit.,* p. 59.
84. IISS, *op. cit.,* p. 20.
85. Mallison and Mallison, *op. cit.,* p. 426.
86. Statement of IAEA Director-General, Mr. Sigvard Eklund, Before the United Nations Security Council on June 12, 1981 on Safeguards *reprinted in* 14 *International Legal Materials* 965 (1981).
87. *Ibid.*

88. *Ibid.*
89. *Ibid.*
90. *Ibid.*
91. *Ibid.*
92. Chant and Hogg, *op. cit.,* p. 59.
93. International Institute for Strategic Studies, *The Strategic Balance 1983–1984* (London: IISS, 1983), pp. 55–56.
94. *Ibid.* Iraq has 70 MiG-23 fighter-bombers. These are the only aircraft that are capable of penetrating Israeli airspace.
95. *Ibid.,* pp. 56–57. Israel has 385 excellent fighter-interceptor aircraft: 40 F-15s, 64 F-16s, 131 F-4s and 150 *Kfirs.* Also, Israel possesses 15 surface-to-air missile (SAM) battalions.
96. Mallison and Mallison, *op. cit.,* pp. 427–429.
97. *Ibid.*
98. *Ibid.*
99. *Ibid.*
100. *Ibid.*
101. *Ibid.*
102. Birnberg, *op. cit.,* p. 86.
103. Mallison and Mallison, *op. cit.,* pp. 435–436.
104. Feldman, *op. cit.,* 125–126.
105. *Ibid.*
106. *Ibid.*
107. *Ibid.,* p. 125.
108. *Ibid.,* p. 123.
109. *Ibid.,* 124.
110. *Ibid.,* pp. 128–134 and 137–139.
111. *Ibid.,* p. 139.

PART THREE

Leadership in Asia

The 1958 Quemoy Crisis and U.S. Leadership

LIN CHENG-YI

I. INTRODUCTION

It is very controversial that Quemoy and Matsu are of strategic value to the United States. According to A. Doak Barnett, the importance of the offshore islands to the Nationalists is primarly psychological. In military terms, although useful to the National- ists as forward posts, they are not essential to the defense of Taiwan. In fact, Barnett thinks the stationing of roughly one-third of the Nationalists' best troops on the islands is probably both unwise and dangerous to the defense of Taiwan itself.[1] To the leaders of the Government of the Republic of China (R.O.C.), keeping troops on Quemoy symbolize that the "civil war" still continues; they can use the islands to blockade the ports of Amoy and Foochow, even wage a war against the People's Republic of China (P.R.C.).

In the United States the mention of Quemoy and Matsu usually evokes one of two extreme reactions; on the one hand the reaction is that the policy is an illustration of U.S. foreign policy at its best. In figurative terms, this is most clearly illustrated by the notion that the U.S. is not going to give up one more square inch of free territory to the Communists. On the other hand, the reaction is that Americans have committed themselves to a policy which rational men would never commit themselves.[2] This kind of con- troversy results in American uneasiness when the said islands are under attack, but when they need American involvement, the U.S. feels that she had not any commitment to these two tiny islands. The first reaction assumes that if Quemoy is taken over by the PRC, the morale of R.O.C. will be shaken, also American allies in East Asia will be depressed. This is the so-called Domino Theory. The second reaction is based on the concept of proximity, it

71

regards the Offshore Islands as belonging to the regime governing mainland China.

In the 1950s, the problem of the Offshore Islands played an important role in Sino-American relations. The Mutual Defense Treaty between the R.O.C. and the U.S., and the Formosa Resolution were the direct outcome of the first Taiwan Straits Crisis (1954-1955). The second Taiwan Straits Crisis (1958) proved to be briefer but more intense than the first. Although in the second Taiwan Straits Crisis the R.O.C. did not lose any territory, in a joint communique with John Foster Dulles, President Chiang Kai-shek lost the right of attacking the mainland positively. The PRC set up the odd-even fire pattern to defuse the crisis. The fire pattern continued until the U.S. and the PRC established their diplomatic relations. The Warsaw Talks also started during the crisis and lasted till 1970.

In Part II of this paper, I will focus on the Sino-American mutual perception just before the crisis. Part III analyzes Chinese tactics during the crisis. Part IV will look at American policy during the crisis. Part V will deal with the limitation on the U.S. when its decisions were being made. Part VI concludes the paper with a review of confrontation and its implication in the Sino-American relations.

II. THE MUTUAL PERCEPTION BEFORE THE CRISIS

China's perception toward the U.S. can be clearly analyzed from Mao's talk with two Latin American leaders in 1956. Then Mao criticized American policy:

> The U.S. is flaunting the anti-communist banner everywhere in order to perpetrate aggression against other countries. The U.S. owes debts everywhere. — The whole world dislikes the U.S. — None of the countries in the East is free from U.S. aggression. The U.S. has invaded our Taiwan Province.[3]

In the 1950s, China's primary enemy was the U.S., who strongly supported Taiwan. In Mao's eyes, the unfinished civil war was obstructed by American occupation in Taiwan. The U.S. was depicted by China as "paper tiger with nuclear teeth." According

Chinese Offshore Islands

to Ralph L. Powell, Mao developed the idea of "paper tigers" to break down the "superstition" that causes people to fear atomic weapons and great powers. The slogan "paper tigers" also is used to help maintain the morale of the Chinese people and armed forces and revolutionaries throughout the world.[4] Mao said,

> Now US imperialism is quite powerful, but in reality it is not. It is very weak politically because it is divorced from the masses of the people and is disliked by everybody and

by American people too. In appearance, it is very powerful but in reality it is nothing to be afraid of, it is a paper
tiger. Outwardly a tiger, it is made of paper, unable to
withstand the wind and the rain. I believe the United
States is nothing but a paper tiger.[5]

After Sputnik was launched, China immediately praised the
achievement of the Soviet Union and was eager to get the nuclear
technology from Moscow. According to the *Peking Review,* China
evaluated:

In the last few years, the Soviet Union has set up the
world's first atomic power station, built the world's first
batch of jet airliners, set up the world's biggest synchron-
tron, launched the world's atomic-powered icebreaker,
manufactured the world's first inter-continental ballistic
missiles, and last but not least, launched the first and
second artificial satellites of the earth. All these feats
proves that in industry, national defense, and certain
important branches of science and technology, the Soviet
Union has surpassed or is catching up with the United
States.[6]

So, Mao and his colleagues came to the conclusion that the Socialist camp had become more powerful than the Capitalist camp. On
the eve of the Moscow Conference in 1957, Mao said to a group of
Chinese students who were attending Moscow University that "At
present, it is not the west wind which is prevailing over the east
wind, but the east wind prevailing over the west wind."[7] In an
agreement on October 15, 1957, the Russians promised to help
China obtain atomic weapons.[8] Without a doubt, Mao calculated
that once he started the Quemoy Crisis, the Soviet Union would
come to aid China with atomic weapons.

Before John Foster Dulles became the Secretary of State, his
attitude toward Communist China was not so hostile as in the days
when he took charge of the State Department. In his book, *War or
Peace* (1950), Dulles wrote:

All nations should be members (of the United Nations)
without attempting to approve closely those which are
"good" and those which are "bad."—If the Government
of China in fact proves its ability to govern China without

serious domestic resistance, then it, too, should be admitted to the United Nations. However, a regime that claims to have become the government of a country through civil war should not be recognized until it has been tested over a reasonable period of time.[9]

China's intervention in the Korean War and the need of support from the Republican legislators on his confirmation as the Secretary certainly changed Dulles' view on the China issue.

Dulles did not change the policy of containment but he did modify the approaches to counter the expansion of communism. He proposed the policy of liberation, massive retaliation, a policy of brinkmanship to President Eisenhower and formulated them into the strategy of "New Look." In implementing the strategy, Dulles depended on the collective security system to contain communism. After the Geneva negotiation in 1954, Dulles believed that the free world would continue to incur defeats unless collective defense arrangements were firmly agreed upon in advance. The Republic of China on Taiwan, therefore, became one of the members in the American West-Pacifican defense perimeter.

In Dulles' memory, the Korean War's nightmare and the imbroglio of Dien Bien Phu were directly manipulated by Peking with the support from Moscow. Since Communist China was the root of upheaval in Asia, the State Department adopted the policy of non-recognition, which meant that the United States did not recognize the legitimacy of Mao's regime. The official reasons of this policy are:

> The generally recognized legitimate Government of China continues to exist and in Taiwan is steadily developing its political, economic, and military strength. Recognition of Communist China by the U.S. would seriously cripple, if not destroy altogether, that government.—Another special consideration in the case of China is that large and influential "overseas" Chinese communities exist in most of the countries of Southeast Asia. The efforts of these countries to build healthy free societies and to develop their communities were to fall under the sway of the Chinese Communist, and a grave threat to Communist subversion through these overseas communities would arise. Recognition of Communist China by the U.S. and the decline in

the fortunes of the Republic of China which would inevitably result—a profound psychological effect on the overseas Chinese that it would make inevitable the transfer of
the loyalties of large numbers to the Communist side.[10]

Although American public opinion was solidly behind the non-
recognition policy (See Table 1), many liberal intellectuals held
quite a different viewpoint. Professor Graebner in his book, *The
New Isolationism,* criticized that U.S. non-recognition of China
had placed the triple burden—military, diplomatic, and intellec-
tual—on Dulles' policy of massive retaliation.[11] Mr. Sulzberger
thought that diplomatic recognition should not be used as a weapon.
He believed that U.S. non-recognition policy had encouraged China's
rapid industrialization with Soviet aid and the mobilizing of its
human forces.[12] However, U.S. non-recognition policy did not
mean that there would be not any contact at all between Washington and Peking. The first Taiwan Straits Crisis (1954–55) drew both
China and the U.S. to the negotiating table in Geneva. It was the
first ambassadorial level talks before the diplomatic relations were
established in 1979. From October 1955 to May 1956, the U.S. and
China exchanged six drafts in solving the tension in the Taiwan
area. Ambassador U. Alexis Johnson, on October 8, 1955, asked
for a declaration from the PRC that she will not resort to the use of
force in the Taiwan Straits area except for defense.[13] The response
from the PRC was that the Taiwan issue was her internal affair,
although she wanted a peaceful resolution to the conflict. That
meant the renunciation of force could not be applied to the crisis.
The Geneva Talks somewhat defused the crisis; nevertheless, the
impasse over the renunciation of force in the Taiwan area finally
led to another crisis in 1958.

III. THE PRC'S TACTICS DURING THE CRISIS

Prior to July 1958 the Taiwan Straits had gone through a period of
relative quiet since the last Chinese Communist probe against the
Offshore Islands in 1954–1955. Periodic artillery fire had been
exchanged between the two sides but at a very low level and most
of it consisted of shells packed with propaganda rather than high
explosives. In addition, the two sides exchanged loudspeaker

TABLE ONE
U.S. Attitudes Toward Dealing with Communist China

	June 1949	April 1950	July 1954	Feb. 1955	Aug. 1955	July 1956	Dec. 1956	Feb. 1957	Jan. 1958	Aug. 1958
Favorable	23	26	8	20	17	11	15	13	17	20
Unfavorable	50	57	79	62	71	74	69	70	66	63
No Opinion	21	16	12	17	12	15	15	17	17	17
No Answer	6	1	1	1	—	—	1	—	—	—

Sources: William P. Hansen and Fred L. Israel, eds., *The Gallup Poll: Public Opinion, 1935-1971*, Vol. Two 1949–1958 (New York: Random House, 1972)

broadcasts across the narrow straits between Quemoy and the mainland, a scant six miles.

According to Charles F. Hermann's definition, the second Taiwan Straits crisis cannot be put in the category of "crisis situation." He would rather put it in the category of "reflexible situation," which means the situation gave the R.O.C. and the U.S. a high threat and not much time to decide on the reaction, but they all perceived a tense situation might erupt in advance.[14] In July 1958 the Lebanon crisis had triggered mass campaigns throughout China's main cities directed against "British and American imperialism in the Middle East." Suddenly, "liberate Taiwan" themes dominated parades and official media. Simultaneously, jet fighters occupied airfields in Fukien and Chekiang which had been completed more than a year earlier but never regularly utilized. Both developments were certain to be detected by American intelligence and thereby constituted a clear warning a full month before the actual attack that trouble was brewing in the Taiwan Straits. A more detailed observation is needed in understanding the intentions of the PRC's military actions.

On July 14 the Iraqi coup took place with a suddenness that certainly surprised the Chinese leadership as much as it did the West. On July 17 the PRC announced the recognition of the new Iraqi regime. On the same day, a rally was held in Peking protesting U.S. intervention in Lebanon. The major address was given by Peng Chen, a member of the Political Bureau of the Central Committee of the Communist Party and Mayor of Peking. In this speech Peng declared,

> At present the US imperialists still occupy by force our territory of Taiwan. We Chinese people are determined

to liberate Taiwan and have full confidence that we will
achieve this. The US forces must get out of the territory
of Taiwan. We firmly believe that the people with justice
on their side will triumph in the end with the east wind
prevailing over the west wind, the imperialists are all the
more definitely doomed to failure.[15]

This speech was the first time that the PRC began to link the "Get
out of the Middle East" campaign with a "Liberate Taiwan"
campaign. On July 25 the *People's Daily* provided its readers with
the first hint of an impending crisis by reporting that the President
of the R.O.C. Chiang Kai-shek on July 17 had cancelled all military
leaves on Taiwan. The article also reported that American planes
had intruded over the mainland and dropped propaganda leaflets
and that there were a number of military meetings going on in
Taiwan.[16] On July 29 the first military engagement of the crisis
took place in the form of an air battle over the Taiwan Straits.
Four R.O.C. F-84 jets on a routine patrol mission were attacked
by four PRC MIG-17's. Two of the F-84's, which were on a photo-
reconnaissance mission, were shot down by the PRC's planes.[17]

On July 31 Soviet Premier Nikita S. Khrushchev arrived unan-
nounced in Peking. There was no mention of Khrushchev's visit to
Peking in the PRC's press until a communique was issued on
August 3 at the conclusion of his visit. On August 4, the *People's
Daily* published the communiqué of the Khrushchev-Mao talks.
The communiqué was notable mainly for its failure to mention
Taiwan and for its lack of substantive content on the Middle East
situation.[18] There is still no reliable information as to what took
place at the meetings between Khrushchev and Mao. Khrushchev
may have cautioned that the Soviet Union was not in a position to
support any offensive operations by the Chinese, but it is extremely
unlikely that he would have vigorously opposed the Chinese plan
to probe the American position in the Taiwan Straits.

On August 13 the *People's Daily* reported that a demonstration
had been held in Amoy against the U.S. and Chiang Kai-shek
because they were creating a tense situation in the Taiwan Straits
by their military build-up.[19] In the week preceding the outbreak of
intensive artillery fire there were no reported air engagements
between the R.O.C. and the PRC, or any shelling of the Offshore
Islands or overflights of Quemoy and Matsu by the PRC. It was

reported later in the *People's Daily* that during the period August 17 through August 30 (which included the first week of the shelling) an enlarged conference of the PRC's Politburo was being held which discussed the formation of the communes and to a lesser extent the creation of the militia.[20] There was thus a week of relative calm before the crisis was to break out into active military action against the Quemoy Islands. This was also a period in which, the R.O.C. and American officials in the field, and at least the lower levels of policy-making in Washington were becoming more and more convinced that a renewed campaign against the Offshore Islands was about to take place.

The PRC's attack began with the firing of some 40,000 shells against the Quemoy Islands on August 23, 1958. The initial fire was directed at a ceremony welcoming the R.O.C.'s Defense Minister Yu Ta-wei to Quemoy. Following this, the PRC, by a combination of artillery fire and patrol torpedo boat action, succeeded in preventing any landing of supplies until American escorted convoys began to sail on September 7. Artillery fire remained heavy during the first two weeks of the crisis and was directed mainly at incoming convoys. At the same time, a number of air engagements took place in which the R.O.C. very quickly demonstrated their superiority over the PRC.

After a month had elapsed without any military or political countermove signalling an American intention to intervene, Mao thought he had given ample warning and received no response, so he launched the bombardment. The PRC's strategy then fully depended on the hope that the U.S. would either stay out or would force a Chinese Nationalist withdrawal from Quemoy. There were several reasons why the PRC may have held to this belief, including the change in the military balance and the U.S. actions in the Middle East. If the U.S. stood by and allowed Quemoy to fall, the R.O.C.'s confidence in the U.S. might be shaken to the point that a deal with the mainland began to seem desirable. Finally, the PRC probably felt that in this period of confidence and of a left move in foreign policy that it should make some kind of effort to seize its most important foreign policy objective—Taiwan. It was clear to China that a direct move against Taiwan was not only militarily infeasible, but also very dangerous and hence that the only hope of getting Taiwan was to put pressure on the Offshore Islands.

Following the successful initiatives, the PRC began to stage political warfare to stablize her military position. The PRC began to beam a series of radio broadcasts at Quemoy, calling upon the garrison to surrender and warning that it was cut off and isolated. On September 4, the PRC announced its claim to a twelve-mile limit, which would put all of the Offshore Islands within her territorial waters. It read as follows:

1. The breadth of the territorial sea of the PRC shall be twelve nautical miles. This provision applies to all territories of the PRC, including the Chinese mainland and its surrounding islands, the Penghu Islands, the Tungsha Islands, the Hsisha Islands, the Chungsha islands, the Nansha Islands, and all other islands belonging to China which are separated from the mainland and its coastal islands by the high sea.
2. The islands inside the baseline, including Tungyin Island, Kaoteng Island, the Matsu Islands, the Paichuan Islands, Wuchiu Island, the Greater and Lesser Quemoy Islands, Tatan Island, Erhtan Island and Tungting Island, are islands of the Chinese inland waters.
3. No foreign vessels for military use and no foreign aircraft may enter China's territorial sea and air space above it without the permission of the Government of the PRC.[21]

The PRC's announcement of a twelve-mile limit was meant as a last warning to the U.S. to get its ships out of the vicinity of Quemoy. It also served the purpose of increasing the political cost to the U.S. of operating close to the Chinese coast. Two days later, Dulles, with the consent of President Eisenhower, issued the famous Newport Statement to make clear to the PRC the American determination to defend Quemoy. It is not overemphasized that the Newport Statement was the first event to help defuse the crisis.

On September 6, the PRC's Premier Chou En-lai issued a statement offering to resume the Sino-American talks. Chou said,

> . . . Now, the US Government again indicates its desire to settle the Sino-American dispute in China's Taiwan area through peaceful negotiation. To make a further effort to safeguard peace, the Chinese Government is prepared to resume the Ambassadoral talks between the two countries.[22]

The Chou statement marked a turning point in the crisis for the PRC and was part of the effort to disengage, but at the same time to adopt a new strategy. On the morning of September 7, the first U.S. escorted R.O.C. convoy set out for Quemoy. The convoy beached in Lialo Bay without interference and with no PRC artillery fire. But two hours after the second convoy reached the beach on September 8, the PRC opened fire with a heavy barrage that prevented the landing of any supplies. When the U.S. made it clear that its intervention would consist of escorting up to three miles, the PRC discovered that their strategy of artillery and patrol torpedo interdiction would be too dangerous, but it was safe to carry out artillery firing against the Offshore Islands. Through the month of September the R.O.C. sent to Quemoy a series of American escorted convoys that came under moderate to heavy Communist artillery fire and, until late in the month, succeeded in landing only very small quantities of supplies. Attempts were also made to land supplies by aerial drop. Several air battles ensued, in which the R.O.C. air force, using the American Sidewinder missiles, outclassed the PRC and destroyed a number of MIGs. The Chinese Communists gradually recognized that they could not hope to effect a blockade of the Offshore Islands simply with artillery fire and therefore it was not worth the military efforts. At the same time, the PRC launched political warfare against the U.S. and the R.O.C.

On September 7, following the unopposed convoy operation by the R.O.C., the PRC issued what was to the first of a series of "serious warnings" about U.S. intrusions into her territory. The warning was released by the NCNA and was against the sending of U.S. ships into the vicinity of Quemoy. The PRC began to criticize American deployment of atomic weapons. Peng Chen, was reported by the *People's Daily* as saying that the US was threatening atomic bombardment.[23] On September 22, the *People's Daily* warned that if the U.S. used atomic weapons against China, it would immediately be subjected to counterblows with similar weapons.[24]

The PRC also opposed the crisis being discussed in the United Nations and the cease-fire proposal. The PRC's Foreign Minister, Chen Yi, ruled out hope for a cease fire and said that the U.S. and the PRC were not at war with each other.[26] By late September, the PRC was apparently becoming worried about the possibilities that the current discussion of the Taiwan Straits Crisis in the General

Assembly would lead to an attempt by some neutral nations to introduce a two-China solution which would involve the R.O.C.'s evacution of Quemoy and Matsu in return for some international guarantee of the status of Taiwan.[27] Chen Yi, on September 5, went further to propose four principles in settling the tense situation:

1. Taiwan and Penghu were Chinese territory.
2. Only the PRC's Government to be the Government of China.
3. All U.S. forces must be withdrawn from Taiwan and the Straits area.
4. The Chinese and the U.S. Governments should settle in peaceful discussions the disputes existing between them.[28]

Under American escort and Communist artillery fire, the Warsaw Talks took place on September 15. During ten meetings in Warsaw (from September 15 to November 5), the PRC issued the order of suspension of their artillery three times, which was not the direct outcome of the Talks. But it cannot be denied that the Talks offered a channel for both sides to defuse the crisis. At the Warsaw Talks, Washington went on to develop its two-stage proposal: first, a formal cease-fire so that real negotiations, not at gunpoint, could be made possible; and second, agreements on specific measures to relieve tensions in the Taiwan Straits, including thinning out of forces, demilitarization, neutralization, trusteeships, or a judicial settlement. It even hinted that a cease-fire and other arrangements could lead to a Foreign Ministers' meeting, as Dulles later intimated publicly.[29] But the PRC focused its proposal on the Taiwan issue. Only after the Americans pulled out from the area, could both sides would settle the problems. To the PRC, the U.S. was occupying her territory, and it was unthinkable for the U.S. to issue a cease-fire proposal on China's property. The PRC accused the U.S. of using the ambassadoral talks to "mask war preparations," to impose a cease-fire to tie Peking hands, and to "plot taking the matter to the United Nations even just as the ambassadoral talks had begun."[30]

While China was against the American cease-fire proposal, on Oct. 6, the PRC Defense Minister Peng Teh-huai announced that there would be a one-week ceasefire if the U.S. ceased to escort the R.O.C.'s convoy. Following the ceasefire, the PRC's propaganda began to stress disputes between the U.S. and the R.O.C. On October 13, the PRC announced that they were continuing the ceasefire for another two weeks. However, on October 20, the PRC announced that they were resuming their fire because an American ship had intruded into her territory waters. On October 25, the PRC said that she was again suspending their fire. This time she declared that she would not fire on even-numbered days against airfields, beaches, and wharves if there were no American escort. President Eisenhower later described this fire pattern as Gilbert and Sullivan's war.[31] It is interesting to look into the reasons why the PRC took the tactics of the cease-fire pattern. Into mid-September, the PRC gradually found that it could not effectively blockade the Offshore Islands, so it was necessary for it to find a step to defuse the crisis. As we mentioned earlier, the PRC could not ignore the possibility of the proposal of two Chinas raised by some neutral countries in the United Nations. Also the PRC should take into account that the R.O.C. might overreact and bomb the mainland. During the crisis, the PRC felt that the Soviet Union was lukewarm in giving its support. In confronting the strongest military deployment in the Taiwan Straits since World War II, the PRC could not fight back with bare hands. The domestic development of the Great Leap Forward was under way, and the expense of heavy artillery became a heavy burden to the PRC. From August 23 to October 4, the PRC had fired 444,433 shells against the Quemoy Islands which cost fifty million U.S. dollars.[32] The PRC also wanted to manipulate the disputes between the R.O.C. and the U.S. in deciding the continuation the of escorts after the cease-fire. The odd-even day fire pattern compelled the R.O.C. government to follow the rule set by the PRC in supplying the Offshore Islands, which was unendurable to Chiang Kai-shek. The PRC thought that Chiang would disagree with American government restraint on him to supply the Offshore Islands on odd days to break the cease-fire pattern.

At the end of October, when the crisis declined, Dulles paid a visit to Taipei and issued a joint communique with Chiang, in which Dulles pressed Chiang for a public statement renouncing the use of force in any attempt to return to the mainland. It was also agreed that there would be a limited reduction of the garrison on Quemoy in return for increased U.S. military power on the

Islands, which I will discuss in the next part of this paper. The *People's Daily* editorial described the communiqué as showing that Chiang only had the right to represent the free China, and made the two-China intrigue more apparent.[33]

IV. AMERICAN POLICY IN THE CRISIS

The U.S. never publicly committed itself to the defense of the Offshore Islands in her agreements with the R.O.C. In the Mutual Defense Treaty between the U.S. and the R.O.C., Article VI stated,

> ... The provisions of Articles II and V will be applicable to such other territories as may be determined by mutual agreement.[34]

The article implied that the treaty can expand to cover the Offshore Islands only after a new agreement was signed by the two governments. Such a mutual agreement was quite impossible and it needed to be sent to the Senate for approval. The Formosa Resolution also did not publicly mention the Offshore Islands, but it later was interpreted by the R.O.C. as the legal base of the American commitment for the defense of the Offshore Islands. The resolution said,

> ... That the President of the US be and he hereby is authorized to employ the Armed Forces of the US as he deems necessary for the specific purpose of securing and protecting Formosa and the Pescadores against armed attack, this authority to include the securing and protection of such related positions and territories of that area now in friendly hands and the taking of such other measures as he judges to be required or appropriate in assuring the defense of Formosa and the Pescadores.[35]

The resolution, according to Townsend Hoopes, was a classic Dullesian contrivance embodying his tendency to sophisticated legalism.[36] It raised the loopholes that if the PRC attacked the Offshore Islands, but had no intention to take over Taiwan, it was doubtful that the U.S. President had the right to apply the resolution to defend the Islands.

Into July 1958, the R.O.C. began to anticipate a Communist move against the Offshore Islands. Urging the U.S. to commit itself publicly to the defense of the Offshore Islands, the R.O.C. also sought modern weapons for its armed forces, including the delivery of American Sidewinder missiles.

Although the U.S. refused to issue a public statement indicating that it would defend Quemoy, it did increase its military assistance to the R.O.C. and began intensive contingency planning for a crisis in the Taiwan Straits. The basic policy of the American government was that it would help defend the Offshore Islands only if necessary for the defense of Taiwan. Before the crisis erupted, a lot of meetings and plans were under way by the Joint Chiefs of Staff and the State Department. One of the plans which was decided by John Foster Dulles on August 22 needs our special observation. It was agreed that the following actions should be taken in order to suggest to both the PRC and the R.O.C. that the U.S. would intervene in the event of a major attack:

1. One carrier should be added to the Seventh Fleet and three carriers should be kept in the Taiwan Straits.
2. A Fleet exercise should be held, but not in the Straits.
3. Admiral Smoot should make a trip to the Offshore Islands.
4. The U.S. should increase its fighters on Taiwan.
5. There should be an increase in the flow of supplies, and if possible, daylight supplies, to the Offshore Islands.
6. There should be a loan of three U.S. LST's to the R.O.C. and the shipping of Sidewinder missiles to the R.O.C.
7. There should be an increase in shipment of weapons to the R.O.C., including recoilless rifles, and other infantry equipment for delivery to the Offshore Islands.
8. There should be a U.S.-R.O.C. joint air defense exercise.[37]

Following the meeting, the exchange of letters between Dulles and the Chairman of the House Foreign Affairs Committee, Thomas Morgan, was arranged. In response to Morgan's letter, which had noted with concern the reports of a Chinese Communist build-up of air power opposite Taiwan and asked for Dulles' comments, Dulles wrote in a letter released on August 23:

> ... I think it would be highly hazardous for anyone to assume that if the Chinese Communists were to attempt to change this situation by force and now to attack and

seek to conquer these islands, that could be a limited operation.[38]

In the letter to Morgan, Dulles had come very far towards satisfying the R.O.C. request that he make a public statement that the U.S. would defend the Offshore Islands. But the letter came a little too late; at the same day the PRC launched the bombardment.

Shortly after the crisis, a White House meeting directed by Eisenhower was held on August 25. A few decisions were made in this meeting. First, in the event of a major attack which seriously endangered the Offshore Islands, it was probable that initially only conventional weapons would be authorized, but prepared to use atomic weapons to extend deeper into Chinese Communist territory if necessary. Second, it was also decided, at the suggestion of the Joint Chiefs, that the American interest in the Offshore Islands would be limited to the holding of Big and Little Quemoy and the five larger Matsu Islands. The decision was made specifically to exclude from the U.S. interest the Islands of Erh-tan and Ta-tan of the Quemoy group and other smaller islands; committing the U.S. to the defense of Quemoy was rejected. It was recognized that such a statement might well contribute to the deterrence, but it was believed that it would complicate America's relations with the R.O.C. and America's allies, as well as complicate the domestic situation in the U.S.[39]

On the second White House meeting after the crisis, Eisenhower went further to decide on the following actions. Despite Chiang's request for his air forces to intrude into the mainland for a counter-attack, Eisenhower approved hot pursuit only in regard to bombing attacks on the principal Islands. It was agreed that escorts would be kept to within three miles of the Islands with the feeling that this should be sufficient to enable successful resupply. It was the legal consideration of not entering the territorial waters of Quemoy. Also once the American escort entered the territorial waters during military operations it would imply a commitment to defend the Islands which, in turn, would imply that the Formosa Resolution had been invoked. The shipment of twelve 8-inch howitzers to the R.O.C. was being expedited, including six with conventional ammunition from Okinawa.[40]

The U.S. effort reached a crescendo on September 4 when Dulles met Eisenhower at Newport, and issued a formal statement.

This action constituted the most important effort thus far to make clear to the PRC the American determination to defend Quemoy. Tsou Tang thought this statement made the U.S. burn the bridge behind it and bring it to the state of brinkmanship.[41] Jan H. Kalicki and Charles A. McClelland thought the statement still did not express American commitment to the defense of the Quemoy Islands.[42] In this formal statement the American government stated that the security of Taiwan had become increasingly related to the security of Quemoy and that the "naked use of force" against Quemoy would threaten the security of the U.S. The statement issued by Dulles after his meeting with the President read as follows:

> ... Any attempt on the part of the Chinese Communists now to seize these positions or any of them would be a crude violation of the principles upon which world order is based, namely, that no country should use armed force to seize new territory. ... Any such naked use of force would pose an issue far transcending the offshore islands and even the security of Taiwan. ... Acquiescence therein would threaten peace elsewhere. ... The US has not, however, abandoned hope that Peiping will stop short of defying the will of mankind for peace.[43]

The statement implied that the U.S. would like to reopen the ambassadorial talks with the PRC. It was quickly responded by Chou by suggesting a talk in Warsaw. When the crisis began to decline, the U.S. became devoted to find a peaceful means to end the crisis. The proposal included the demilitarization in the Offshore Islands, mutual renunciation of force, using the good offices of Secretary-General Dag Hammarskjold, and discussion of the issue in the United Nations.

On the same day when the U.S. began to escort Nationalist China's convoy to Quemoy, in his phone conversation with the Special Assistant to the Deputy Secretary of Far Eastern Affairs, Marshall Green, Dulles indicated for the first time interest in the possibility of an agreement aiming at the demilitarization of the Offshore Islands. This proposal received strong opposition from Green, and Walter S. Robertson, Deputy Secretary of Far Eastern Affairs, and some military men. Green felt demilitarization was inadvisable as it would heighten acceptance of the two-China concept. Robertson responded that demilitarization was not a practical solution since the Communists could seize the Islands at any time after they were demilitarized.[44] The proposal was killed but it later was modified into the reality of troop reductions from Quemoy. In his September 30 news conference, Dulles exhibited uncharacteristic flexibility on the Taiwan Straits issue. He not only confirmed that his Government had "no commitment of any kind" to help Chiang return to the mainland, but he also implied that the administration would favor reducing R.O.C. forces on Quemoy and Matsu if the Communists agreed to a cease-fire in the Straits. In the bluntest public statement yet to emerge from a high American official, Dulles told the press, "if there were a cease-fire in the area which seemed to be reasonably dependable, I think it would be foolish to keep these forces on these islands. We thought that it was rather foolish to put them there."[45] Just only after the crisis, Dulles finally achieved the goal of troop reduction on the Quemoy Islands.

The mutual renunciation of force between both sides of the Taiwan Straits was based on the concept that the PRC was not the only one to blame, the R.O.C. should also refrain from any provocative actions against mainland. This was the effort which the U.S. representatives undertook in the Warsaw Talks. On September 18, at the second session of the Warsaw Talks, Dulles instructed Ambassador Jacob Beam to present the proposal to the Chinese Communists, which stated, "the United States renounces the use of force in the area of the Quemoy Islands and the Matsu Islands except in individual and collective self-defense. The U.S. will seek that Quemoy Islands and the Matsu Islands will not be used for attacks or other provocative actions directed against the mainland or other coastal islands."[46]

During the crisis, Dulles was interested in handing the issue to the United Nations. The result of American public opinion, to some extent, strengthened Dulles' decision to use the means of peaceful settlement through the United Nations. (See Table 2). Dulles thought that the Quemoy crisis was not just a civil war of China, it also endangered international stability. Dulles mentioned in the press conferences on September 18 and 30 that he was determined to reserve the right to hand the issue to the United Nations if the Warsaw Talks proved a failure.[47] Dulles urged Secretary-General Dag Hammarskjold play the role of good offices in the crisis, but Hammarskjold rejected the proposal for there had not much chance of success.[48]

TABLE TWO
U.S. Public Opinion on the U.N. role in the Taiwan Straits Crisis

Interview Date 9/10–15/58

This question was asked of those who said they had been following the crisis over Quemoy and Matsu: Would you like to see the United States work out a solution to this problem in the United Nations before we get more involved in a military way in the fight over these two islands?

Yes	91%
No	6
No opinion	3

Interview Date 9/10–15/58

The next question asked those aware of the situation was: It has been suggested that Formosa be neutralized—that is, put under the protection of the United Nations. Do you think this is a good idea or a poor idea?

Good idea	61%
Poor idea	19
No opinion	20

Sources: William P. Hansen and Fred L. Israel, eds., *The Gallup Poll: Public Opinion, 1935-1971,* Vol. Two 1949-1958 (New York: Random House, 1972), p. 1569.

When the Chinese Communists issued the extension of the cease fire for another two weeks, Dulles arrived at Taipei under the heavy artillery launched by the PRC to protest his visit to Taiwan. After a three-day visit in Taipei, Dulles and Chiang argued but finally reached the following communique:

> The Government of the Republic of China declared its purpose to be a worthy representative of the Chinese people and to strive to preserve those qualities and characteristics which have enabled the Chinese to contribute so much benefit to humanity. The two Governments reaffirmed their dedication to the principles of the Charter of the United Nations. They recalled that the treaty under which they are acting is defensive in character. The Government of the ROC considers that restoration of freedom to its people on the mainland its sacred mission. It believes that the foundation of this mission resides in

the minds and the hearts of the Chinese people and that
the principal means of successfully achieving its mission
is the implementation of Dr. Sun Yat-sen's three people's
principles and not the use of force.[49]

According to Chief of Staff of the Army, General Maxwell Taylor,
who was then also in Taipei, the major achievement of the communique lay in the words, "not the use of force."[50] But from the
viewpoint of the R.O.C., it denied having given up the right to use
force under the conditions that there was a revolution in the
mainland, or Taiwan was under attack. Eisenhower thought the
R.O.C. actually had given up the right to wage an aggressive war
against mainland China.[51] The R.O.C. was not only winning the
title of "a worthy representative of the Chinese people", they also
gained a guarantee from the U.S. to strengthen the firepower on
Quemoy to compensate for a troop reduction from the Quemoy
Islands. The text of the formal agreement, reached by General
Wang Su-min, the R.O.C.'s Chief of Staff, and General Leander
Doan, the chief of the U.S. Army Military Assistance Advisory
Group, read as follows:

With respect to military defense of the Offshore Island
Complexes of Quemoy and Matsu, the undersigned agreed
as follows:

1. continued improvement of forces;
2. existing counter-battery artillery capability be augmented
   as follows:
   a. Quemoy complex—a minimum of 12 (additional) 240
      mm howitzers, and a minimum of 12 (additional) 150mm
      guns;
   b. Matsu complex—240 mm howitzers and 4 more when
      available, 1 battallion of 155 mm guns, when available;
   c. Further study of need for more;
   d. Lacrosse missile considered at a later date;
3. armor strength on Quemoy augmented:
   a. a minimum of 1 tank battalion;
   b. a study of tank strength;
4. services and combat support units will not be increased and
   will be reduced if possible.

5. reduction of forces on Quemoy will include 1 infantry division and 1 additional division and/or individual so that there shall be a net reduction of not less than 15,000 men with a target date of 30 June 1959 for completion.[52]

Under the PRC's fire pattern and the R.O.C.'s consent to withdraw her troops from the Offshore Islands, the crisis nearly came to an end. On November 1958, the Berlin Crisis again raised the tension between the West and the East. The second Taiwan Straits conflict was over, but its outcome was far from definitive. The Taiwan and the Offshore issue is still not resolved in Sino-American relations up to the present.

V. LIMITATIONS ON AMERICAN DECISION MAKERS

There was some danger that events might have spiraled out of control in the Quemoy crisis of 1958, because this was a crisis in which a good deal of actual violence was employed and because the direct protagonists were client states who had some interests in dragging in their superpower protectors.[53] But the pressure from her allies and domestic politics, contrained the U.S. from the brink of war. On the other hand, Russian reluctance to give substantial support to the PRC also helped to let Mao cool down and defuse the crisis.

American policy during the crisis was contrained by four factors. Contraint 1 was to hold Quemoy. Contraint 2 was to avoid war. This involved restraining the Formosan ally, who was urging and asking for permission to make various military moves that could easily lead to escalation, involvement of the Soviet Union and war. Constraint 3 was set by soft-line Senate opposition and the British ally. It was two-fold: do not alienate Britain and do not give the Senate opposition a propaganda opportunity. Constraint 4 was maintaining alliance solidarity with Chiang. The problem therefore was to devise a strategy that would be firm to Chinese Communists, accomodative for the U.S. public and Britain, restraining and yet supportive of the Formosan ally. The U.S. must firmly commit itself to defend Quemoy in the eyes of the Chinese (constraint 1) but must not do so in the perceptions of the US Senate (constraint 3) because this would give the Senate critics an opening—Eisenhower was not authorized to defend Quemoy unconditionally. The U.S. must demonstrate military support for Chiang (constraint 4) but must not do so (constraint 2) in such a way to encourage him.[54]

It needs our further look at the opposition from the American Democratic party and its ally—Britain. Just after Dulles' Newport Statement on September 5, former Secretary of State Dean Acheson sounded an alarm, "We seem," he said, "to be drifting, either dazed or indifferent, toward war with China, a war without friends or allies, and over issues which the administration has not presented to the people, and which are not worth a single American life."[55] Senator John F. Kennedy also stated that the U.S. should continue its defense of Taiwan but it was unwise to get in the entanglement of the Offshore Islands.[56] Much of the criticism came from members of the Senate Foreign Relations Committee and from other congressional leaders. Senator Theodore Francis Green, the Chairman of the Foreign Relations Committee, on September 29, wrote the President to express his "deep concern that the course of events in the Far East may result in military involvement at the wrong time, in the wrong place, and on issues not of vital concern to our own security."[57] Nevertheless, the Democrats, on their side, also faced a delicate problem of trying to determine how far they could properly go in criticizing the Quemoy policy without violating the accepted bipartisam principle that politics should stop at the water's edge. Their reservations about Quemoy were genuine. On the other hand, they did not wish to be accused of torpedoing the national foreign policy for reasons of electoral advantage.[58] Therefore, in the decision-making process during the crisis, it was the White House, not the Congress, that played a dominant role.

Far back to the first Taiwan Straits Crisis, former British Prime Minister Winston S. Churchill was worried about American involvement in a war with Communist China.[59] Also Prime Minister Anthony Eden, speaking in the House of Commons on January 26, 1955, drew a careful distinction between the Government's attitude towards Taiwan, he said, "which during the present century had never legally belonged to China," and the Offshore Islands, which "had always been regarded by us as a part of China." He went further to say that he would like to see the Nationalists withdraw their forces from the coast island.[60]

Throughout the crisis the British Government made clear its opposition to American policy. American officials met frequently with British officials in an effort to explain and justify the American positions.[61] But it was apparent that the British viewpoints were quite different from those of the U.S. The British thought the primary crisis was on Quemoy, but the secondary crisis might erupt in Hong Kong.[62] The British obliged by sending a battalion to Hong Kong and two more carriers to their Far East fleet—despite their considerable skepticism, even disapproval, of U.S. policy.[63]

The basic policy of the British Government can be traced as follows. In a letter responding to Secretary Dulles, Prime Minister Harold Macmillan stated that a small war was not likely to continue long and the use of nuclear weapons seemed possible. Macmillan asked whether the United Nations General Assembly or the Security Council could do anything.[64]

On September 11 British Foreign Secretary Selwyn Lloyd in a letter to John Foster Dulles said that the Western line of defense, including Taiwan, was weakened by the R.O.C. retention of Quemoy and Matsu. He cautioned that if the defense of them involved even the use of tactical nuclear weapons, the risk of a chain reaction was obvious. The letter asserted that R.O.C. withdrawal would strengthen the R.O.C. position and might be the only way to avoid defeat. Selwyn alluded to the importance of the Warsaw Talks and suggested the value of talks at a higher level. In concluding, Selwyn indicated that the United Kingdom was opposed to the American policy of defending the Offshore Islands, but said that the United Kingdom was willing to make a trial balloon of any idea if the U.S. thought it would help and concluded finally by asking how the United Kingdom could help.[65]

While Washington acted to keep London informed and took Britain opposition as a sign of widespread dissent of American policy, the British position did not, as should be clear, have any specific direct effect on the U.S. policy.

Altough the Russian policy during the crisis was very cautious, the U.S. was worried that the escalation of conflict might give China an excuse to invoke the Sino-Soviet Treaty into effect and impel the Soviet Union to provide atomic weapons to China. To fight a nuclear war for Quemoy was not in the Russian and American interest.

On September 5, 1958, a *Pravda* "observer" article noted statements in the American press to the effect that Washington might use tactical nuclear weapons against the China mainland and might issue a warning that the U.S. Government would not exclude the issue of atomic arms by American forces in the Far East. It replied that:

> The Chinese People's Republic has sufficient strength to counter the aggressors fully.[66]

Khrushchev's first letter to President Eisenhower came on September 7, after the Newport Statements and the Warsaw Talks proposal were issued. The Soviet criticism of the U.S. since then became stronger and stronger as the crisis began to defuse.[67] In Khrushchev's first letter, he stated:

> The Chinese people wants peace and defends peace but it does not fear war. If war will be thrust on China, whose people are full of determination to defend its rightful cause, then we have not the slightest doubt that the Chinese people will give a worthy rebuff to the aggressor.[68]

Khrushchev also warned the U.S. that:

> An attack on the Chinese People's Republic which is a great friend, ally and neighbor of our country, is an attack on the Soviet Union. True to its duty, our country will do everything in order together with People's China to defend the security of both states, the interests of peace in the Far East, the interest of peace in the whole world.[69]

Khrushchev did not mention the Sino-Soviet Treaty, nor did he intend to offer nuclear weapons to the PRC. On the contrary, Khrushchev put much emphasis on the notion that the PRC alone can stand bravely against the U.S., he dropped a hint to the PRC that it was unwise for her to stir the U.S. to use the atomic bomb.[70] Tang Tsou thought this letter went far beyond the vague wordings of the Sino-Soviet Treaty of Friendship and Alliance of 1950.[71]

The second letter was issued on September 19, when the Warsaw Talks began and the use of atomic weapons became less probable in the Taiwan Straits. Khrushchev bluntly declared,

> ... Those who harbor plans for atomic attack on the Chinese People's Republic should not forget that the other side too has atomic and hydrogen bombs and appro-

priate means to deliver them, and if the Chinese People's Republic falls victim to such an attack, the aggressor will at once suffer a rebuff by the same means. ... We have a Treaty of Friendship, Alliance, and Mutual Assistance with this great friend, ally and neighbor of our country, ... and let no one doubt that we shall fully honor our commitments.[72]

The letter was the first time in the crisis the Soviet Union mentioned the possibility of applying the 1950 Sino-Soviet Treaty in the Taiwan area. But the verbal help did not come along with the substantial support. When 10 MIGs were shot down by Nationalists with Sidewinders, the Soviet reaction was very circumspect.

On October 5, Khrushchev, in an interview with a reporter of *Tass,* was more cautious in mentioning the Treaty. He said the Treaty could only be applied when the PRC was attacked by the U.S. It implied that the American defense for the Offshore Islands was not a necessary condition for the Treaty to come into effect.[73]

Therefore we can come to the conclusion that during the crisis, only verbal support the Soviet Union did offer. However, the Soviet restraint helped to defuse the crisis. There was hardly any buffer between Chinese and American forces, and both Taipei and Peking refused to play the proxy roles of the French and Vietnamese in Indochina. Soviet inhibitions seemed to fulfill the crisis control roles vacated by the buffers and proxies of other crises. According to Jan H. Kalicki, the second Taiwan Straits Crisis is the first to offer lessons on the prospects for world order after the breakdown of Cold War bipolarity.[74]

VI. CONCLUSION

According to *Long Live of Mao Tse-tung Thought,* Mao on September 5, 1958 admitted that in planning the bombardment of Quemoy and Matsu, "he simply did not calculate that the world would become so disturbed and turbulent."[75] Up to the present, we still have not seen any information which shows that Mao was challenged in his decision-making in the crisis. Mao's thinking on the principle of "despise the enemy strategically, respect him tactically" did imply testing American intentions and strength before committing his forces in the crisis. Basically Mao miscalculated the situation from two facets. He launched the bombardment, only to see Washington respond with alacrity. Mao was also expecting military assistance from the Soviet Union, however, he was disappointed by the lukewarm response.

The PRC did not lose the game totally, she set up the odd-even day fire-pattern for the Nationalists to follow, she also speeded her endeavor in developing her own nuclear deterrence. Tension also permitted the PRC to "mobilize the troops, the backward strata, and the middle factions to rise in struggle" through their "fear of fighting an atomic war."[76]

During the crisis, the U.S. was interested in defending an abstract principle of international conduct—that international boundaries cannot be changed by the use of force. This was a major consideration in dealing with the Taiwan Straits Crisis. But under the pressure from the Congress and the allies, the U.S. could not but refrain herself from the brink of war, and impose restraint on the R.O.C. The U.S. had not consented to the R.O.C. bombardment of the mainland. They suspended the escort when the cease-fire order was issued by the PRC. America's most successful manipulation, during the crisis, was to restrain Chiang from waging an aggressive war against Communist China and his agreement not to use force in the future.

Charles A. McClelland thought that it was via tacit bargaining, and not the Warsaw Talks, which defused the crisis.[77] The R.O.C. was not allowed to bombard the coastal artillery bases, while the PRC only used the artillery fire in the crisis. American escort was limited to the three miles away from Quemoy, while the PRC stopped using patrol torpedo boats to harass the convoy. After the U.S. pressed the R.O.C. to denounce the use of force, the PRC issued her odd-even day fire pattern. Due to the tacit interaction, the Sino-American confrontation quickly declined.

Jan H. Kalicki illustrated that the Taiwan Straits crisis (1958) represents the most satisfactory model of Sino-American crises behavior and interaction, for they became self-limiting without requiring either buffers or proxies to blunt unilateral escalation or mutual misapprehension.[78]

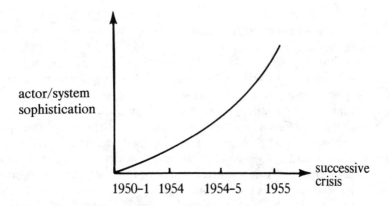

Learning Curve of US–PRC Crisis Handling

Sources: Jan H. Kalichi, *The Pattern of Sino-American Crises* (Cambridge: Cambridge University Press, 1975), p. 217.

Kalicki thinks that Korea, 1950–1, was undoubtedly the low point in the curve because of its intra-war crises. Indochina, 1954, occupied an intermediate position as, on the one hand, a relatively salutary crisis experience in terms of indirect Sino-American participation and, on the other hand, as the representation of mutual misapprehension regarding the character and extent of Sino-American commitments.[79]

During the crisis, as tough figure as Dulles, even gave the PRC a hint in the possibility of holding foreign ministers' talks. It reminded us of what Khrushchev said to Dag Hammarskjold, "Dulles invented brinkmanship but he would never step over the brink."[80] After Dulles passed away, the American policy toward the PRC became more flexible than before. A policy of rapproachment was pursued by Kennedy and Johnson, but the door to China was still not opened. A breakthrough of Sino-American relations was finally achieved after the next Republican, Richard Nixon, became the President of the United States.

On November 7, 1969, the U.S. quietly ended the 19-year presence of the 7th Fleet in the Taiwan Straits. On October 11, 1974, the Formosa Resolution was formally repealed by the U.S. Congress. The Mutual Defense Treaty between the R.O.C. and the U.S. was rescinded, because of the establishment of diplomatic relations between Peking and Washington. In the 1979 Taiwan

Relations Act, the U.S. promised to provide Taiwan with arms of a defensive character, and consider any boycott or embargo of Taiwan to be of great concern to the U.S. But in the Communique of August 17, 1982, the U.S. stated its intention to gradually reduce its sale of arms to Taiwan. To date, the PRC has never promised to renounce the use of force in the Taiwan Straits. It is highly unlikely that the PRC will invade the Offshore Islands, because it will jeopardize China's relations with the U.S. If the crisis occurs again, the best the U.S. could do is to provide advanced weapons to Taiwan and let the Chinese solve their own problem. To strengthen the defense of Taiwan and Pescadores, it is necessary for National-ist China to reduce the number of its troops in the Offshore Islands. The Nationalist leaders realize that only by acquiring the more advanced weapons, can they have more bargaining power to maintain the status quo and survive in another Quemoy Crisis.

NOTES

1. A. Doak Barnett, *Communist China and Asia* (New York: Harper, 1960), p. 414.
2. Don E. Kash, "United States Policy for Quemoy and Matsu," *The Western Quarterly,* Vol. 16, No. 4 (December 1963), p. 912.
3. *Selected Works of Mao Tse-tung,* Vol. 5 (Peking: Foreign Language Press, 1977), p. 308.
4. Ralph Powell, "Great Powers and Atomic Bombs are Paper Tiger," *The China Quarterly,* Vol 23, No. 3 (July–September 1965), p. 60.
5. *Selected Works of Mao Tse-tung,* Vol. 5 (Peking: Foreign Language Press, 1977), p. 310.
6. *Peking Review,* Vol. 1, No. 3 (March 18, 1958), p. 7.
7. *People's Daily,* November 20, 1957.
8. William E. Griffith, *The Sino-Soviet Rift* (Cambridge: MIT Press, 1964), p. xi.
9. John Foster Dulles, *War or Peace* (New York: Macmillan Company, 1950), pp. 190–91.
10. Hungdah Chiu, ed., *China and the Question of Taiwan* (New York: Praeger, 1973), p. 278.
11. Norman A. Graebner, *The New Isolationism: A Study in Politics and Foreign Policy since 1950* (New York: The Roland Press Company, 1956), p. 181.
12. C. L. Sulzberger, *What's Wrong with U.S. Foreign Policy* (New York: Harcourt, Brace and Company, 1959), p. 194.
13. Kenneth T. Young, *Negotiating with the Communist: The United*

States Experience, 1953-1967 (New York: McGraw-Hill, 1968), p. 414.
14. Charles F. Hermann, "International Crisis as a Situation Variable," in James N. Rosenau, ed., *International Politics and Foreign Policy* (New York: Free Press, 1969), p. 418.
15. *People's Daily,* July 18, 1958.
16. *Ibid.,* July 25, 1958.
17. *Ibid.,* July 30, 1958.
18. *Ibid.,* August 4, 1958.
19. *Ibid.,* August 13, 1958.
20. *Ibid.,* September 1, 1958.
21. *Ibid.,* September 5, 1958.
22. *Ibid.,* September 7, 1958.
23. *Ibid.,* September 8, 1958.
24. *Ibid.,* September 22, 1958.
25. *Ibid.,* September 30, 1958.
26. *Ibid.,* September 21, 1958.
27. Morton A. Halperin, *The Taiwan Straits Crisis of 1958* (Santa Monica: The Rand Corporation Research Memorandum, 1966), p. 328.
28. *Ibid.,* pp. 330-31.
29. Kenneth T. Young, *op. cit.,* p. 184.
30. *Ibid.,* p. 180.
31. Dwight D. Eisenhower, *The White House Years: Waging Peace, 1956-1961* (New York: Doubleday, 1965), p. 304.
32. Hungdah Chiu, *op. cit.,* p. 171.
33. *People's Daily,* October 1958.
34. Hungdah Chiu, *op. cit.,* p. 251.
35. *Ibid.,* p. 257.
36. Townsend Hoopes, *The Devil and John Foster Dulles* (Boston: Little Brown and Company, 1973), p. 273.
37. Morton A. Halperin, *op. cit.,* p. 94.
38. *The Department of State Bulletin,* Vol. 39 (September 8, 1958), p. 379.
39. Morton A. Halperin, *op. cit.,* pp. 113-122.
40. *Ibid.,* pp. 197-206.
41. Tang Tsou, *The Embroilment over Quemoy: Mao, Chiang and Dulles* (Salt Lake City: University of Utah, 1959), pp. 15-22.
42. Jan H. Kalicki, *The Pattern of Sino-American Crisis* (Cambridge: Cambridge University Press, 1975), p. 191. Charles A. McClelland, "Decisional Opportunity and Political Controversy: the Quemoy Case," *Journal of Conflict Resolution* 6 (September 1962), p. 209.
43. Hungdah Chiu, *op. cit.,* pp. 279-80.
44. Morton A. Halperin, *op. cit.,* p. 409-412.
45. *The New York Time,* October 1, 1958.
46. Morton A. Halperin, *op. cit.,* p. 451.
47. *The New York Times,* September 19 and October 1, 1958.

48. Morton A. Halperin, *op. cit.,* p. 439.
49. Hungdah Chiu, *op. cit.,* pp. 287-88.
50. Morton A. Halperin, *op. cit.,* p. 532.
51. Dwight D. Eisenhower, *op. cit.,* pp. 303-4.
52. Morton A. Halperin, *op. cit.,* p. 542.
53. Glenn H. Snyder and Paul Diesing, *Conflict among Nations* (Princeton: Princeton University Press, 1977), p. 238.
54. *Ibid.,* p. 239.
55. Richard P. Stebbins, ed., *The United States in World Affairs, 1958* (New York: Harper, 1959), p. 320.
56. Morton A. Halperin, *op. cit.,* p. 392.
57. *The State Department Bulletin,* Vol. 39 (October 20, 1958), pp. 605-6.
58. Richard P. Stebbins, *op. cit.,* p. 122.
59. Dwight D. Eisenhower, *op. cit.,* p. 609.
60. Evan Luard, *Britain and China* (Baltimore: The John Hopkins University Press, 1962), p. 170.
61. Morton A. Halperin, *op. cit.,* p. 457.
62. *The Economists,* September 20, 1958, p. 912.
63. Glenn H. Snyder and Paul Diesing, *op. cit.,* p. 445.
64. Morton A. Halperin, *op. cit.,* p. 461.
65. *Ibid.,* pp. 462-63.
66. *The Current Digest of the Soviet Press,* Vol. 10, No. 36 (October, 1958), p. 9.
67. Alice Langley Hsieh, *Communist China's Strategy in Nuclear Era* (Englewood Cliffs: Prentice-Hall, 1962), p. 124.
68. *The State Department Bulletin,* Vol. 39 (September 29, 1958), pp. 499-503, *The New York Times,* September 9, 1958, p. 12.
69. *The New York Times,* September 9, 1958, p. 12.
70. John R. Thomas, "Soviet Behavior in the Quemoy Crisis," *Orbis,* Vol. 6, No. 1 (Spring 1962), p. 53.
71. Tang Tsou, "Mao's Limited War in the Taiwan Straits," *Orbis,* Vol. 3, No. 3 (Fall 1959), p. 346.
72. *The New York Times,* September 20, 1958, p. 1.
73. *The Current Digest of the Soviet Press,* Vol 10, No. 40 (November 12, 1958), p. 18.
74. Jan H. Kalicki, *op. cit.,* p. 205.
75. Allen S. Whiting, "New Light on Mao—Quemoy 1958: Mao's Miscalculations," *The China Quarterly,* No. 62 (June 1975), p. 266.
76. *Ibid.,* p. 269.
77. Charles A. McClelland, *op. cit.,* p. 203.
78. Jan H. Kalicki, *op. cit.,* p. 203.
79. *Ibid.*
80. Frank J. Merli and Theodore A. Wilson, eds., *Makers of American Diplomacy: From Theodore Roosevelt to Henry Kissinger* (New York: Charles Scribner's Sons, 1974), p. 287.

U.S. Strategic Policy Toward Occupied Japan

SHAW FAWN KAO

I. INTRODUCTION

As the Second World War entered into its last year, a vital transformation in the structure of international relations in the Asia-Pacific region emerged. Japanese imperialist expansion and its contraction had not only shaken the foundation of the European colonial empires in Southeast and East Asia, but had also provided an opportunity for reassertion of power by China and the Soviet Union. Japan, then, was about to be defeated, and its far-flung domination demolished. The United States was now the predominant power in the Western Pacific, and its influence was felt among Chinese, Koreans, Vietnamese, and others struggling for sovereignty. And yet most of these developments were the consequence of the war against Japan, and military expediencies had dictated America's responses to them. How far the U.S. was going to involve itself in Asian affairs, and what roles it was to play in the whole region, were questions that had not been systematically dealt with except for two things: One was to defeat Japan and to cripple permanently Japan's militarism and imperialism; the other was to create a powerful and friendly China as a new Asian stabilizer.[1]

The Yalta Conference, convened in February 1945, can be characterized as the occasion when an attempt to define U.S. interests was achieved. It was here that the heads of the three greatest powers—namely, Churchill, Roosevelt, and Stalin—met and reached a number of crucial decisions which would determine the shape of the postwar world for years to come, and which, in fact, laid a foundation for what later developed as the Cold War. The Yalta agreements signified the readiness of the three powers to come to some basic understanding on the nature of their interrelationships after the War and the way in which each would play a role in postwar world politics. In Asia and the Pacific the Conference established the trusteeship system for the mandate territories held by the enemy, thereby assuring American control over the Pacific islands that were seized from Japan. The Soviet Union for its part, was formally guaranteed the retrocession of the Kurile Islands and South Sakhalin Islands in the event of its entry into the Pacific War. Thereby, the U.S. would remain the dominant power in the Pacific and exercise the greatest control over Japan after the war, while the Soviets would reestablish its predominant position in Northeastern Asia.

Based on the Yalta framework, the Americans certainly believed that they had firmly established amicable relations with the Soviet Union and that the Big Three would cooperate well to reestablish the post war international order. However, the American dream of postwar peace and Big Three cooperation was to be shattered as the Soviet Union expanded into Eastern and Central Europe. The Yalta framework was eroded further in Asia by the establishment of the Communist regime in China, as well as Korean War, and the Communist Chinese intervention in it. The series of events that damaged the equilibrium would force the U.S. to continuously adjust its strategic policy in Asia. And accordingly, U.S. policy in Japan would have to be modified from a defensive policy against Japan to a friendly in order to revitalize Japan and bring it into the United States military alliance.

The overriding global strategy of the U.S. to maintain the balance of power in Asia and to contain effectively the Communist aggression from the Asian Continent dictated the formulation of U.S. strategy in the Pacific.

II. THE EARLY STAGE OF THE OCCUPATION: 1945-1947, A PERIOD OF A PUNITIVE REFORM POLICY TOWARD JAPAN AND THE UNCERTAIN STRATEGY TOWARD ASIA

A. A Strategy Of Defense Against Japan

The most significant characteristic of the occupation of Japan was that it did not constitute a "military government" by the allied forces. Japan, unlike Germany, was not divided into zones of occupation but was treated as a whole organism. Moreover, in Germany the occupation authorities established a new regime in which the Germans became its mere functionaries, retaining important roles only in local government and administration. In Japan, the basic framework of government and bureaucracy was kept intact. Although the country was effectively disarmed and the top military and civilian leaders arrested and purged, the bulk of the bureaucrats stayed in their jobs—including officials of the central government, the policemen, and the public school teachers. Most important, General MacArthur, the head of Supreme Commander for Allied Powers (SCAP), decided to keep the Emperor system. This decision was derived from the view that the occupation of Japan could be carried out much more smoothly by keeping the Emperor as the head of state and using his authority for purposes of the occupation, rather than risking confusion and possible resistance to the occupation authority which may have resulted from purging the Emperor. Paradoxically, because the Emperor system was kept and chaos avoided, and also because the United States did not share power with others in Japan, it was possible to carry out some of the punitive-reform programs designed by the U.S. toward Japanese society with greater success.

Based on the Initial Post-Surrender Policy, the U.S. had set two goals as the guidelines for the occupation of Japan, one of which was the Demilitarization, and the other being the Democratization of Japan. Under the policy of Demilitarization, the Japanese would have to totally disarm themselves. They were also to suffer the trial and the punishment of war criminals; the disarmament of Japanese Armed Forces, and the destruction of its war industries. In addition, the U.S., based on the Yalta framework, was to cooperate with the Soviet Union's usurpation of a number of Pacific islands which had been occupied by the Japanese during the war. Of these islands the most crucial for the Soviets in term of long range strategic and political implications were the Kuriles and South Sakhalin, and Okinawa and Bonin for the U.S. The purpose of such actions was to circumscribe Japanese sovereignty to within only its four main islands.

The policy of Democratization was a positive aspect for constructing a domestic Japan. It was implemented through a number of political and social reform programs. Economically, the U.S.

adopted Edwin Pauley's reparations proposal to eliminate Japanese war potential. The methods of elimination were the destruction of the top-heavy industry structure; the removal of wholesale manufacturing plants, and transferral of surplus goods of Japanese industrial potential to Japan's neighbors. These actions were taken by the U.S. with the intention of enabling Japan's neighbors to resist Japan's potential economic control over them and for them to resist any attempt of renewed Japanese military aggression.[2] Hence, the objectives of such policies were to make certain that Japan could never again become a menace to the peace and security of the world. Furthermore, in so doing it was an effort to transform Japan from a warlike, aggressive state ruled by authoritarian militarists into an unarmed peaceful nation, with a responsible democratic government.[3]

It was obvious that during this early period in the post-war Asian area, the main focus was on China. The U.S. was hoping that a strong and democratic China, functioning as a regional stabilizer, would play a leading role in protecting the postwar peace in the Far East, and that China would function as a deterrent to the Soviet Union's aggression, as well as Japan's potential threat to Asia. From the U.S. strategic viewpoint, Japan would have to be reestablished under U.S. guidelines as a pro-U.S. entity. Therefore, the strategy of the U.S. in this period was to provide for defense against Japan, not defense for Japan—a strategy of preventing a future attack by Japan.

B. The Early Proposal For A Peace Settlement

The changing situations in Europe and in the Pacific in 1946 and 1947 demonstrated that the Yalta system still provided the basic framework for the development of international relations. But some partial changes had transpired that were of vital significance during this period. Instead of developing a partnership in maintaining peace and stability in the world, the U.S. and the Soviets gradually came to view each other through a lens of hostility and mutual distrust. The axiom of "cooperation" disappeared from the dialogue of the two power relationship. Instead, the rubric of confrontation and containment were now used to make sense out of what appeared to be happening. On the international scene, the "cold war" replaced "cooperation and understanding" as a conceptual framework to discribe American-Soviets relations.

Despite the hostile mood, there was little thought of military confrontation with Russia, and no program existed for a massive build-up of the U.S. armed forces in the Asian-Pacific area. Nor that Japan should be transformed once again to a military power. Such a step would be a serious infringement on the framework of the American-Russian balance in the Asian-Pacific region. Actually, the Soviets were extremely sensitive to any sign that Japan's demilitarization and eradication of imperialism were not moving fast enough. In 1947 they repeatedly accused the MacArthur administration of having failed to carry out these program fully and even of having planned to resurrect the Japanese army. American authorities were well aware of the source of Soviet concern, but they, too, did not wish to drastically alter the status quo. There was only one thing that some American officials, including MacArthur, believed it possible to do, and that was to work toward reducing and removing ultimately all foreign troops from Japan, so that Japan would maintain a truly peaceful existence.

In early March of 1947, General MacArthur called for the start of a series of non-punitive treaty talks to be held in the near future, for the withdrawal of the U.S. forces from Japan upon its independence, and UN supervision of the country following a settlement. Mr. George Atcheson, who was then the political advisor in Japan, reported to President Truman that "General MacArthur has remarked to me several times that there inevitably comes a time when a military occupation no longer serves its purpose and becomes a deterrent to its own objectives."[4] MacArthur further proposed that Japanese security be guaranteed by the U.S. forces in Okinawa and South Korea. He believed that an air force in Okinawa would be enough to deter Soviet air and naval units already lacking sufficient fuel and numbers for an assault on Japan.[5] MacArthur's assumption was that Japanese security, under the terms of the new constitution, would be subject to the justice and the good faith of the peace-loving people of the world. It was incumbent, therefore, that the Allied nations, for their part, undertook to guarantee the neutrality of Japan with a view to the transfer of such an undertaking to the stewardship of the UN where this responsibility should properly rest. However, General Robert L. Eichelberger, then the Commander of the U.S. 8th Army in Yokohama, strongly disagreed

on this type of idealistic policy toward Japan. He felt that the base
in Okinawa could not replace U.S. troops in Japan. He said, "I
can't see how they can take troops out of Japan until the communist question is settled. We can't afford to let Russian or Japanese
Communists get control of this country."[6] The Policy Planning
Staff, led by George Kennan and organized to formulate cold war
strategy, also saw the great risks in an early relinquishment of
Allied control over Japan. The Policy Planning Staff insisted on
U.S. strategic trusteeship of the Bonins, Volcano and Marcus Islands.
In addition, the Staff suggested proceeding in the negotiations on
the assumption that the U.S. will require military facilities in
Okinawa. As to whether American base facilities would be required
on the Japanese main islands, the Staff did not take a position at
that time. In fact, the Staff have "no evidence that facilities for
land forces or for air forces alone on this territory would serve
any useful purpose."[7] Therefore, it was obvious that the Staff did
not consider this moment propitious for a final decision on this
subject.

C. The Uncertain Policy On Security Matters

For Japan the year of 1947 had tremendous significance. Not only
because the Japanese Socialist Party won the first time in the national
Diet election, but also because the new constitution was promul-
gated, declaring the nation's renunciation of "war as a sovereign
right of the nation and the threat of force as means of settling
international disputes." And furthermore, the Soviet Union, at this
juncture, rejected a Conference of eleven powers who were members of the Far Eastern Commussion for Japanese peace settlement.

Even since the beginning of the post war world, the Japanese
Foreign Ministry had begun to prepare for the peace settlement. In
Tokyo's view, once the Japanese achieved the goals of the "Potsdam
Declaration", the Allied Powers had pledged to make peace with a
"peace-loving Japan."[8] The growing Cold War tension between the
Soviets and the U.S. since 1946 had never infringed upon this
perception in Japan. The Japanese assumed that regional tensions
would not prevent international cooperation. Most important, some
top Japanese officials, especially Mr. Yoshida, believed that the
Cold War could provide an opportunity for inducing the U.S. to

restore Japanese independence, while at the same time maintaining its force in Japan for security purposes. In other words, Japan would regain sovereignty through a peace treaty, but its national security would be safeguarded primarily through the presence of American forces.[9] Such an idea fitted the "no-war" constitution, reinforced the notion of peaceful economic expansion, and rationalized the strategy of maintaining close economic, political, and military ties with the United States.

However, the existing situation was not exactly coincident with Japanese idealistic assumptions. In early 1947 in Washington, the Hugh Borton Group, which had been established in October 1946 to produce a State Department's draft, pursued three objectives in relation to a treaty with Japan: First, it worked to include the Soviets in the Peace Treaty; secondly, the group sought to safeguard the American strategic monopoly in Japan under the guise of Allied cooperation; and finally, it proposed to keep the Japanese military weak and peaceably inclined. Nevertheless, on July 22 the Soviet Union turned down the first Conference for a Japanese peace settlement proposed by the U.S. Charles Bohlen, the counselor of the State Department, analysed the reason for the Soviet attitude and said it "was their fear that the Yalta Agreement giving them the Kuriles and the South Sakhalin would be upset at an eleven-power meeting at which they could be outvoted."[10]

On August 29, Secretary of State George Marshall's second invitation once again was turned down by the Soviets. Therefore, in early September, the U.S. decided to postpone the Conference and allow the Policy Planning Staff to determine whether it would be in the interest of the U.S. to have a peace treaty with Japan without the participation of the Soviet Union. The postponement decision was then also enhanced by the Staff's study on the question of a Japanese peace settlement. The study indicated that it had no satisfactory evidence that Japanese society would be politically or economically stable if turned loose and left to its own devices at this stage. If Japan was not politically and economically stable when the peace treaty was signed, it would, warned the Staff, be difficult to prevent communist penetration.[11] Mr. Kennan further perceived that cooperation with the Soviet Union was unlikely, and that American policy should be to prevent Japan from falling under Soviet control.[12]

In short, in 1947, a constructive phase of the peace settlement was initiated. But, the Japanese security questions as well as her future role in the Asian international system had not been clarified at this juncture, as Mr. Atcheson described in the late 1947 saying "the question of Japanese security policy has not yet become a realistic issue, nor have we formulated with any degree of concreteness our own objectives with respect to Japan and the Pacific area."[13] It, therefore, explicitly indicated that the U.S., at this stage, had not clearly defined her strategic objectives in the Asian-Pacific region.

III. A TRANSITIONAL PERIOD OF THE U.S. STRATEGY FROM UNCERTAINTY TO A CLEAR DEFENSE LINE: 1948-1950

A. The Relaxation Of Punitive Economic Policy Toward Japan

1948 was the year that the Cold War entered its new stage. In February, Czechoslovakia sank into the Communist bloc; on March 20, the Soviets withdrew from the Allied control council; on June 23, the Berlin Blockade began. These unstabilized situations, in addition to the U.S. presidential campaign, had initially shifted the U.S. attention away from Japan. But the war in China and Vietnam, the growing frustration of a heavy tax on the U.S. citizens, and the Republicans as well as many U.S. business sectors beginning to condemn the U.S. policy toward Japan as socialization, sparked U.S. reconsideration of East Asia.

Initially, the U.S. punitive economic policy toward Japan dictated that the Japanese be allowed only a minimum standard of living and that everything else be taken away from them for reparations. Consequently, in the winters of 1945 to 1946 and 1946 to 1947 the Japanese were saved from starvation only by food shipments from the United States military stores.[14] General MacArthur pointed out that Japan was becoming a burden on the American taxpayer, who was not yet used to such burdens. And even more serious, he argued, was the fact that the social disorder and the despair resulting from these terrible economic conditions were threatening to undermine his efforts to remake Japan into a stable, responsible democracy.[15] George Atcheson also recommended to President Truman to rebuild Japanese economic ability and foreign trade. He said: "It is necessary for the accomplishment of our overall objectives and is in the interest of the American tax-payer who otherwise foots the bill."[16] These external as well as internal factors pushed forward and caused the punitive economic policy toward Japan to begin to relax. There were two reports that significantly influenced the U.S. policy at this stage. The Strike Report recommended that except for primary war facilities, production facilities which would be used effectively in Japan would not be subject to reparation removal. And the Johnston Report went a step further, suggesting that instead of a reform-punishment program which continued to feed the Japanese at the cost of $400 million annually to the American taxpayer, the primary war facilities which could be used in a peacetime economy be retained by the Japanese.[17] The U.S. economic strategy obviously needed Japan to stand on her own feet.

In Tokyo, Mr. Yoshida was pleased by this tilt toward economic growth. But he supposed that all programs seemed to assume a prolongation of Japan's occupied status. In his view, the U.S. version of economic reconstruction meant "peacetime stability without peacetime independence."[18] It was true indeed that the U.S. government continued to assume that it enjoyed a dominant position in Japan in accordance with the Yalta understanding. In the absence of overt Soviet moves to challenge that supremacy, it was not surprising that American officials stressed economic recovery as the most practical way of maintaining the Yalta status quo in Japan or in the Pacific.

B. The Strengthening Of The U.S. Position in Japan

The changing environments in the year of 1948 caused the Yalta system's framework for dealing with Asian policy to be no longer tenable. The hope that a friendly China would maintain some sort of balance of power in the Far East was dashed by the communist advance. Americans, then, would have to pursue the other possibility to cope with this situation, that was the policy of strengthening its own position within its sphere of predominance. This approach had become more and more articulate in the U.S. policy toward Japan during 1948 and 1949.

Although certain key officials in the State Department, including George Kennan, were not totally convinced that China was falling into the Soviet orbit, virtually all were in agreement that the United States must improve its military position in the Western Pacific to prevent further disintegration of the Yalta equilibrium. Obviously, Japan, due to her potential industrial power, her highly educated population, and her strategic location, would be a key in any such arrangements, and a new concept of Japanese-American relations had to be developed. In a forthright policy recommendation, Mr. Kennan wrote in February 1948 that the United States should:

> ... devise policies toward Japan which would assure the security of that country from communist penetration and domination as well as from military attack by the Soviet Union and would permit Japan's economic potential to become once again an important force in the affairs of the area, conducive to peace and stability.[19]

On March 25, Kennan also recommended peace treaty postponement to the State Department. In Kennan's view, indefinite delays would permit the U.S. to blunt the edge of radical reforms that were strengthening an alien influence in Japan. He further judged that American demilitarization policies had left Japan more easily swayed by the Soviets, whose forces were located only miles away in the Kuriles and Sakhalin.[20] Such a view reflected Kennan's thinking that continued poverty, weakness, and insecurity of Japan would contribute an element of instability to the Asia-Pacific region. It was imperative, therefore, that Japan be permitted once again to become a positive factor in the international affairs of the area. And the postponement at this time would permit America to rework these reforms, in addition to strengthening the economy, and to reversing the disarray so conducive to communist advance.

At the same time, Japan was also ready to cast its lot with the U.S. in the Cold War. In return, Foreign Minister Ashida Hitoshi was suggesting that the U.S. guarantee Japan against a Soviet attack or invasion. But Mr. Ashida was not proposing that the U.S. assume complete responsibility for Japan's security. He was, rather, asking the U.S. to guard Japan's external security, while his government took care of internal security. Japan, dimilitarized and economically prostrate, could not be expected, for the foreseeable future, to build military forces capable of repelling a Soviet attack. The Government would have all it could do to build up its domestic police forces, on the ground and on the sea, in order to protect Japan against insurrection and infiltration.[21] The Japanese seemed to believe that Japan's strategic value to the U.S., along with their willingness to assume complete responsibility for the internal communist threat, and their desire to cooperate with the U.S. in defending Japan against Soviet attack would constitute a realistic and reasonable basis for a mutual defense arrangement. Mr. Ashida and Mr. Yoshida before him were planning to provide for Japan's security by becoming an ally of the U.S., not a military dependency.

C. The Definition Of The Strategic Defense Line

Since mid-1949, the National Security Council, in view of the serious international situation created by the Soviet Union's policy of aggressive communist expansion, recommended the Government not to press for a peace treaty at this juncture.[22] The Joint Chiefs of Staff (JCS) further enhanced the NSC's viewpoints and claimed that a peace treaty, from the military point of view, would be premature at the present time. According to the JCS's assumption the continuing Soviet policy of aggressive communist expansion made it essential that Japan's democracy and western orientation first be established beyond all questions, and that global developments were still in such a state of flux that measures leading to the risk of loss of control of any area might seriously affect American's national security.[23] The JCS also acknowledged that Japan was of high strategic importance to U.S. security interests in the Far East, primarily because of her geographic location, her manpower as well as her industrial potential. If Japan were to be taken under the USSR's control, Japan could be used as a base for aggressive action aimed directly against U.S. bases in the Western Pacific, and step-by-step advances eastward and to the Southeast Asia region. Furthermore, under the USSR's control, Japan probably would provide both the arsenal personnel and the manpower for aggressive military campaigns in the Pacific and the Southwest.[24]

The State Department, however, would not totally share the JCS's opinions. In their view, the threat to Japan in these circumstances came not from direct attack and invasion, but from agitation, subversion and a coup d'etat.[25] The threat was that of a conspiracy inspired by the USSR, but conducted by Japanese. The State Department also emphasized that Japan depended not only on the military capabilities and intentions of the U.S., but also on the attitude—the orientation—of the Japanese people. Therefore, the only hope for the preservation and advancement of such democracy and pro-U.S. orientation as now existed in Japan lay, suggested the State Department, in the early conclusion of a peace treaty with that country.[26] The dramatic rise in the Japanese Communist party's representation from 4 to 34 seats in the general election in early 1949 seemed to be used as a strong evidence by the State Department for the need of an early peace settlement.

Although the Joint Chiefs of Staff and Secretary of Defense Louis Johnson opposed the terms of peace for Japan, they did offer two conditions that would make a treaty acceptable to them: First, if the State Department could obtain the Soviets and PRC's signature to a final accord, they would agree to support a settlement. They reasoned that a treaty concluded without the Soviets, in particular, would allow it to harass or invade Japan on the pretext that the legal state of war had continued; second, the peace treaty stipulated several security requirements, including the U.S.'s right to maintain military forces in Japan and the strategic trusts over the Okinawa, Mariana, and Marshall islands.[27] Because the Soviets would never sign such a peace settlement, Mr. Johnson and the JCS reaffirmed their view that "negotiations now leading toward a peace treaty with Japan are still premature."[28] In response toward the JCS's reasons for opposition, Mr. Acheson offered to meet the JCS security demands by supporting the right to garrison troops, and, if necessary, the right to move freely in Japan. As for the Communist's signatures, Mr. Acheson argued that future Soviet actions would be prompted less by legal considerations than by existing political and power relations between the U.S. and the Soviets.

No matter what the differences within the government on the issue of peace treaty, the vast majority of American policy makers at this moment, recognized the importance of Japan's security in connection with U.S. Asian strategy. In early January of 1950, Mr. Acheson explicitly emphasized that "the defense perimeter runs along the Aleutians to Japan and then goes to the Okinawa . . . and runs from the Okinawa to the Philippine Islands."[29] Thus, it was at this time that the U.S. government definitely defined its strategic boundaries along the eastern coast of the Asian continent for the containment of Soviet expansion. And for the preventing of such aggression, the U.S. would require air and naval bases in Okinawa, the Philippines, the Aleutians, and Midway. Six months later, this concept of the island-chain strategic boundaries was further enhanced by the outbreak of the Korean War.

IV. THE KOREAN WAR AND THE EMERGENCE OF A NEW RELATIONSHIP BETWEEN THE U.S. AND JAPAN

A. The Sino-Soviet Alliance And The U.S. Proposal On Japanese Rearmament

By the end of 1949 any idea of the Soviet Union and Communist China joining together with the U.S. to conclude a peace treaty with Japan was becoming not only unrealistic but undesirable from the American point of view. In order to preserve the American position in the Western Pacific, the best strategy seemed to be to put an end to the state of war, and then to conclude a military alliance with Japan, and enable the U.S. to keep its forces on Japanese soil. At the same time, the U.S. had tried to push Japan for rearmament. More specifically, the National Security Council recommended the formation of a 150,000-plus national police force in Japan.[30]

Just as the Americans believed the Yalta equilibrium was being eroded through the communist victory in China, the Russians and the Chinese Communists became convinced that Japan was being turned into a tool of U.S. imperialism. After 1949 they reiterated with increasing frequency that the U.S. was secretly rebuilding a Japanese army and that the reactionaries and militarists in Japan were scheming once again to invade the Asian Continent. In order to oppose the ambitions of the American imperialists and the Japanese militarists, the Chinese people must, as Communist General Chu Teh mentioned in July 7, 1949, strengthen their friendly alliance as the most important weapon to resist the new aggression in East Asia.[31] As if to act out such a scenario, Mao Tse-Tung left for Moscow at the end of the year and signed a treaty of "friendship, alliance, and mutual assistance" with the USSR on February 1950. In the U.S.'s view, the Sino-Soviet alliance was clearly aiming at the U.S.-Japan current relationship. So in late June of 1950, when John Foster Dulles, then special consultant to Secretary of State Dean Acheson, visited Japan for the formulation of the peace treaty, he concluded that Japanese rearmament was inevitable. He told Mr. Yoshida that only an arrangement on defense could prevent Japan from falling prey to Soviet and Communist Chinese advances.

Mr. Dulles' assignment on foreign affairs at this point was signaling a return to the bipartisanship of U.S. foreign policy, suspended in the aftermath of the presidential election of 1948, and in the Far East where American foreign policy continued to be criticized by the Republicans, who claimed they had not been consulted as they had on European problems.[32] Initially, Mr. Dulles was given nothing specific to do in the State Department. But from his observation he realized that the State Department was making no progress in several directions because too many people had to agree before any positive action could be taken. He told Secretary Acheson that:

> You'll never get anything done unless you select someone in whom you have confidence, give him a job to do, and then hold him to results. Look at the Japanese Peace Treaty—the Department has been discussing it for four years without result. Why don't you give action, with the understanding that if he can't do it, he fails? Give him a target and enough authority to get there.[33]

Mr. Acheson was impressed by Mr. Dulles' suggestion, and soon afterward he assigned Mr. Dulles to take over the handling of the treaty.

According to John Allison, director of the Office of Far Eastern Affairs (he was then also Mr. Dulles' assistant), Mr. Dulles had an exaggerated fear of what the Soviets wanted to do and were going to do. He steadfastly believed the Soviets were aiming at world

conquest, and took literally the proclamation by Joseph Stalin's in
"The Problems of Leninism" that the road to Europe was through
Asia . . . The Sino-Soviet Friendship Treaty made him especially
nervous.[34] Other factors underlying Dulles' support for rearmament included his belief that the Senate would never approve an
indefinite defense commitment and his feeling that military depen-
dence would obstruct political independence. Despite his convic-
tion on rearmament, however, Mr. Dulles did not then envisage a
specific level of Japanese buildup. According to Allison, Mr. Dulles
"evidently favored something over 100,000 troops."[35]

On June 25, 1950 when the Korean War broke out, the post-war
Yalta equilibrium in the Far East was being further eroded by the
Communist attack on South Korea. The U.S. had positive reasons
to redefine the structure of Asian-Pacific international relations on
the principle of the revitalization of Japan once again as a new
Asian stabilizer, and the use of the Japan Islands as the base for
U.S. troops for Korea. Prime Minister Yoshida, therefore, tried to
use this new situation as the bargaining chip to strengthen his
opposition on Japan's rearmament. Yoshida's reason was that Japan
was neither economically nor psychologically prepared to rearm.
He argued that the National Police Reserve, which had been
formed of a 75,000-man force by MacArthur to prevent domestic
turmoil in the absence of the bulk of the U.S. occupation forces
that had to be sent to Korea, represented the maximum contribution Japan could make to its own defense. General MacArthur also
agreed that Japan's rearmament would be inappropriate and
suggested a military contribution of the old arsenals and idle
facilities belonging to the Japanese army and navy. MacArthur
contended this policy would help the U.S., whose own armament
had been delayed since the war, also providing a boost to the
Japanese economy.

Despite MacArthur's and Yoshida's remarks, Dulles remained
unconvinced about the virtues of an unarmed Japan. In Dulles'
view, events in Korea clearly overrode the General's objections to
Japanese rearmament. He felt that the North Korean's attack sig-
naled the Soviet Union's attempt to control the manpower and
industrial resources of Japan and that such control over Japan (and
Germany) would permit the Soviets to sustain and win a long war
against America.[36] In Dulles' estimate, the difficulty with Japan
was its distance from the U.S. and its proximity to the Soviets.

Dulles believed that the U.S. could not protect Japan singlehanded, it would need help from the Japanese themselves.

B. The Chinese Intervention And The Idea Of Collective Security With Japan

After Communist China intervened in the war in early November, the bad situation deteriorated further. When Mr. Dulles returned to Washington, immediately after the Korean War had broken out, he believed that peace with Japan was even more necessary than before. The two departments came to a decision when the Secretaries of State and Defense signed a memorandum, which was endorsed by President Truman on September 8, 1950, that "the United States should now proceed with preliminary negotiations for a Japanese Peace Treaty."[37] The President then assigned Mr. Dulles as his official representative, with the rank of Ambassador, to handle the matter.

However, almost immediately the progress of a peace settlement with Japan was upset by full-scale Chinese Communist intervention. Dulles later wrote that "Developments in Asia confirm that there is a comprehensive program, in which the Soviet and Chinese Communists are cooperating, designed as a present phase to eliminate all Western influence on the Asiatic mainland, and probably also in relation to the islands of Japan, Formosa, the Phillippines, and Indonesia."[38] Secretary of State Acheson even perceived that "it is probable that a principal objective is Japan, the industrial and human resources of which nation have for many years been dominant in Asia, and which, if added to the resources now possessed by the Soviet Union would greatly alter the balance of power in the world to the disadvantage of the U.S. and its allies."[39] To meet this situation, Acheson suggested that the U.S. had to commit substantial sea and air power to the defense of the Japanese island chain. Dulles proposed a further step to "use Taiwan as a base for covert and perhaps open Chinese activities against the China mainland, which would at least divert the Chinese Communist Government." In addition, Dulles mentioned the "possibility of stimulating guerrilla and insurrectional activities within areas of Soviet control so as to divert them from external advantages to the problem of attempting to consolidate an already overextended position."[40]

As to the Japanese security problems, Dulles knew that it meant looking in two directions. The first direction flowed from the postwar threat of aggression from Soviet-Communist expansion in Asia. The U.S. had positive reasons for not wanting Japan's industrial potential gathered within the Iron Curtain and integrated with the resources of Manchuria, and thus made available to help provide the communist world with the kind of economy which could underwrite a long war and possibly win it. In view of this, the U.S. could be counted on to support the sea and air power to protect it. The second direction flowed from Japan's aggression which led to the war and from the fear of the victims of Japanese aggression concerning its possible resurgence in the future. So, security at this juncture meant giving assurance to nations which had been occupied or threatened by Japan that the latent enemy would be prevented from rebuilding an aggressive military machine.

For long-term security, Dulles, with the recently concluded NATO in mind, was a strong advocate of a collective regional security, which he had opposed before the Korean War. In April 1950, he felt a formal arrangement would commit stronger and more responsible nations to support unstable and irresponsible members, and would suggest to the Communists that they could expect no U.S. opposition in countries excluded from the arrangement.[41] But the North Korean attack and especially the Communist Chinese intervention changed the strategic ball game. In his view, the U.S. security interests required "a Pacific Pact composed initially of Japan, Australia, New Zealand, the Philippines, the United States and perhaps Indonesia."[42] He argued that Japan's safety was dependent on the peace and stability of the Far East, and that Japan should contribute positively to the defense of the entire region. The U.S. would also be willing to cooperate in the defense of Japan if Japan immediately began taking vigorous measures to defend itself and would agree to participate militarily in collective regional security. He did not believe that Japan was economically and psychologically incapable of rearming.

Dulles also felt that a tie between Japanese military units and a Pacific Pact would minimize domestic opposition to a Tokyo defense effort. In his view, the Korean situation had awakened the Japanese from their postwar stupor. But he believed the Japanese people still opposed rearmament and would accept bases only as a necessary last resort for defense. Dulles judged that "a Pacific Pact, authorized by Article 51 of UN Charter, would internationalize Japanese forces and thus ease reconciliation with the present [no-war] constitution."[43]

C. The Peace Settlement And Japan's Reentering The International Family

It was a manifestation of the Cold War in general and the Korean War specifically that Japan regained her independence through the San Francisco Peace Conference. By late January of 1951, it was apparent that the Chinese attack had not been decisive. Mr. Dulles, being eager to get things rolling again, made his second trip to Tokyo to seek a peace settlement. Mr. Dulles' approach to the peace settlement stemmed from his experience as a young man at the Versailles Peace Conference of 1919. As a member of the American delegation he had witnessed the writing of a vengeful peace which built up resentment in Germany which Hitler was able to exploit and which led to World War II.[44]

"You can have one of two kinds of peace," Mr. Dulles said, "One is a Carthaginian peace, which is cruel, ruthless, inflexible, and must be enforced with military strength for a long time. It is a peace that can tolerate no infractions whatever. The other is a peace based on the belief that human nature is capable of regeneration; that if it fails at times, it is capable of a better way of life. This kind of peace is one of magnanimity based on power."[45] Mr. Dulles continued: "We want the kind of peace that has a good chance of making Japan and the United States close associates in the future. It can not be done without the free will of the conquered. It must be a peace of reconciliation."[46]

It was with this philosophy that Mr. Dulles approached his task. The next problem was one of procedure. The traditional way to write a treaty was to call an international conference—but that would involve Soviet Union's rejection by her veto power. Moreover, during the years of inaction, a new complication had been added to the Far Eastern power situation: The newly emerged Communist China had been recognized by seventeen nations, though not

by the U.S. It raised seemingly insuperable problems of recognition for a conference. Dulles thus decided to proceed through diplomatic channels, which meant that the U.S., taking the lead, would confer separately with the other allied nations. And further, the U.S. should proceed with as many as possible of its friendly allies in order to spread the burden of responsibility and to minimize the adverse effects of Soviet-Communist pressures upon the Japanese.[47]

After intensive negotiations, on September 8, 1951, the U.S. and Japan finally signed a peace treaty and mutual security treaty in San Francisco. Thereafter, a new relationship, or we might call a new partnership, emerged between the two countries: the rearmament of Japan, continued presence of the U.S. forces in Japan, their military alliance, and the retention by the U.S. of Okinawa and the Bonin Islands. In return, the U.S. would remove all restrictions on Japan's economic affairs, and renounce the right to demand reparations and war indemnities. Simultaneously, the U.S. would offer a mutual assistance pact to Australia and New Zealand, pledging that the U.S. would regard an attack on either of them an attack on itself.

As to the issue of rearmament, the Japanese government under Mr. Yoshida steadfastly refused to undertake a large-scale rearmament, desiring instead to concentrate on economic recovery and to rely on a mutual defense treaty with the U.S. to safeguard national security. The result was a compromise of a 50,000-man National Defense Force. The figure of 50,000 was really nonsense. According to a General Headquarter's estimate, defense of the home islands required a force of at least 325,000 men. Anyhow, the U.S. accepted, as one American official put it that: "The 50,000-man was better than nothing but inadequate."[48] The Americans evidently consoled themselves that they got the Yoshida's promise but not the figure.

Therefore, Japan was identified once again by her position in the Asian international community by becoming a member of the American security system. The Soviet Union and Communist China, however, could not be expected to accept the legality of the new system and insisted that as far as they were concerned the state of war with Japan still remained. China, in fact, was not represented at the San Francisco Conference. And the American view was that Japan should be free to conclude a separate peace treaty with the

Chinese government of its choice. But it was evident that Japan really had no choice in the matter, as Dulles exacted a promise from Yoshida that the Japanese government would sign a peace treaty with the Republic of China in Taiwan. The 1952 peace treaty between Japan and ROC was an anomaly insofar as the authority of the Nationalists was limited to Taiwan and its environs. Japan recognized the situation that the provisions of the treaty would be applicable only to those areas under control of the ROC. In other words, the conclusion of a peace treaty in such circumstances was tantamount to accepting the view that there existed two Chinese governments, one in Peking and another in Taipei. Whatever the merits and the detriments of these situations, the fact remained that by refusing to invite Peking to the peace conference and by inducing Japan to sign a separate treaty with Taiwan, the U.S. was further revealing its policy of isolating Communist China and entrenching its own power on the island. It thus increased the tension between China and the U.S. And it could be seen as the byproduct of the Korean War.

Another crucial development since the Korean War was the extensive U.S. involvement in Indo-China and other parts of Southeast Asia. This was related to the broader Cold War perception, calling for a reactive response to any Communist movement. Thus, Japan would reenter into Southeast Asia through the pathway of the San Francisco peace settlement. The Japanese government also recognized that because of her identification with the U.S. containment policy, Japan could not revive the kind of close trade relations with mainland China which it had heavily maintained before the war. Southeast Asia would then provide a substitute market and source of raw materials. Therefore, the more stable the region became due to American power, and the more American aid was poured in, the more favorable the situation would be for Japan.

V. CONCLUSION

Looking back over the origin and development of the U.S. postwar strategic policy toward occupied Japan, it seems clear that this policy had been changed predominently by the influence of the U.S.-Soviet rivalry, and more especifically by the broader Cold

War perception—the response to contain any Communist movement.

At the close of the Second World War, American Far Eastern policy was primarily directed toward the creation of a free, unified, democratic China which would take her place, as had been planned at the Cairo Conference of 1943, among the great powers devoted to maintaining world peace as well as Asian stabilization. Simultaneously, the U.S. was, based on the Yalta understanding, undertaking a punitive policy toward defeated Japan. The U.S. strategy was then to defend against Japan, not defense for Japan. And there was no thought at all that Japan should be able to transform itself as an Asian power.

After the erosion of British power in postwar affairs, it turned to the U.S. to assume part of its geo-political functions. It brought about a face-to-face confrontation between American and Soviet power in Europe and the Middle East. Thereby, it increased Cold War tension everywhere around the world. And in Asia, the balance of power of the Yalta framework was damaged by the emergence of the Communist China, and further by the Sino-Soviet alliance. Eventually, the U.S. decided to revitalize Japan once again as a power replacing China to fill into the power vacuum in the Asia-Pacific region.

The Korean War and the Communist Chinese intervention only made a bad situation worse. The American decision-makers perceived it as a comprehensive program of Communist aggression and perhaps indicatory of a direct objective toward Japan. In view of this, the U.S. insisted on supplying the sea and air power to prevent Japan from falling into the Communist bloc and to speed up the conclusion of a peace treaty and the rearmament of the country.

Therefore, it was obvious that the U.S. strategic policy toward occupied Japan since the postwar period was a policy of maintaining the Yalta equilibrium of international relations in this region. To help the Japanese to regain their independence was the first step of the U.S. strategy to cope with the erosion of the Yalta system of the balance of power by the Communist aggression in Asian continent. Later, the U.S. involvement in Taiwan, Indo-China and other parts of Southeast Asia were all following this conceptual framework. But China's growth as a more independent power, the development of the Vietnam War as well as many other changing situations within the region made this strategy, based on the Yalta's equilibrium, become more unrealistic. However, it was not until the emergence of the Nixon Doctrine in the 1970s that a replacement for this Cold War strategy and a reshaped international strategy toward a new kind of balance of power in the region was achieved.

Finally, this study also suggests that for the Japanese a bit of the Cold War might not be such a bad thing. It was the Cold War that turned Japan from a conquered and occupied country to an independent entity. It was the Cold War indeed that made Japan reenter the international community and start on its path to economic recovery, prosperity, and expansion.

NOTES

1. John Spanier, *American Foreign Policy Since World War II.* (New York: CBS College Publishing, 1983), p. 53.
2. Jerome B. Cohen, *Japan's Economy in War and Reconstruction.* (Minneapolis: University of Minnesota Press, 1949), p. 419 and 420.
3. Raymond Dennett and Robert K. Turner (ed.), *Documents on American Foreign Relations, 1947.* (New Jersey: Princeton University Press, 1949), p. 97.
4. "Atcheson's report to President Truman on June 19, 1947." In *Foreign Relations of the United States.* 1947, p. 233.
5. Michael Yoshitsu, *Japan and the San Francisco Peace Settlement.* (New York: Columbia University, 1982), p. 15.
6. Ibid., p. 15.
7. "Memorandum by the Director of the Policy Planning Staff (Kennan), October 14, 1947." In *Foreign Relations of the United States.* 1947, p. 540.
9. Akira Iriye, *The Cold War in Asia.* (New Jersey: Prentice-Hall Inc., 1974), p. 148.
10. "Memorandum by the Counselor of the Department (Bohlen) to the Under Secretary of State (Lovett), August 12, 1947." In *Foreign Relations of the United States.* 1947, p. 487.
11. "Memorandum by the Director of the Policy Planning Staff (Kennan), October 14, 1947." In *Foreign Relations of the United States.* 1947, p. 233.
12. George F. Kennan, *Kennan Memoirs, 1925-1950.* (Boston: Little, Brown and Company, 1967), p. 368-396.
13. "Kennan to Lovett (Under Secretary of State), August 12, 1947." In *Foreign Relations of the United States.* 1947, p. 486 and 487.
14. Shigeru Yoshida, *Yoshida Memoirs.* (Boston: Houghton Mifflin Company, 1962), p. 204-206.

15. Martin E. Weinstein, *Japan's Postwar Defense Policy, 1947-1968.* (New York: Columbia University Press, 1971), p. 14.

16. "The Political Adviser in Japan (Atcheson) to President Truman, January 5, 1947." In *Foreign Relations of the United States.* Vol. VI. 1947, p. 159.

17. "Secretary of State to Certain Diplomatic Offices, April 27, 1949." In *Foreign Relations of the United States.* 1949, p. 717-720.

18. Michael Yoshitsu, op. cit., p. 26.

19. George F. Kennan, op. cit., p. 381.

20. "Report by the Director of the Policy Planning Staff (Kennan): Recommendation with Respect to U.S. Policy Toward Japan, March 25, 1948." In *Foreign Relations of the United States.* 1948, p. 681-719.

21. Martin E. Weinstein, op. cit., p. 20.

22. "Report by the National Security Council on Recommendations with Respect to United States Policy Toward Japan (NSC 13.1), May 6, 1949." In *Foreign Relations of the United States.* 1949, p. 730.

23. "Report by the Joint Chiefs of Staff: Strategic Evaluation of United States Security Needs in Japan (NSC 49), June 1949." In *Foreign Relations of the United States.* 1949, p. 776.

24. Ibid., p. 774.

25. "Department of State Comments on NSC 49, June 15, 1949." In *Foreign Relations of the United States.* 1949. p. 871-873.

26. Ibid., p. 871-873.

27. Michael M. Yoshitsu, op. cit., p. 29 and 30.

28. "Memorandum by the JCS to the Secretary of Defense, December 22, 1949." In *Foreign Relations of the United States.* 1949, p. 922 and 923.

29. McGeorge Bundy, ed., *The Pattern of Responsibility.* (New Jersey: Augustus M. Kelley • Publishers, 1972), p. 199 and 200.

30. Akira Iriye, op. cit., p. 174.

31. Ibid., p. 175.

32. Louis L. Gerson, "John Foster Dulles." In *The American Secretaries of State and Their Diplomacy.* Vol. XVII. edited by Robert H. Ferrell. (New York: Cooper Square Publishers, Inc., 1967), p. 55 and 56.

33. John R. Beal, "Bull's Eye for Dulles." In *Harper's Magazine.* Vol. 203. No. 1218., November 1951, p. 89 and 90.

34. "Memorandum of Conversation by the Special Assistant with the Secretary, April 7, 1950." In *Foreign Relations of the United States.* 1950, p. 1165.

35. Michael M. Yoshitsu, op. cit., p. 41.

36. "Memorandum by Dulles to Acheson, July 19, 1950." In *Foreign Relations of the United States.* 1950, p. 1243 and 1244.

37. "Draft Memorandum for the Secretary of Defense, December 13, 1950." In *Foreign Relations of the United States.* 1950, p. 1386.

38. "Paper Prepared by Mr. John Foster Dulles, Consultant to the Secretary of State, November 30, 1950." In *Foreign Relations of the United States.* 1950, p. 162.
39. "The Secretary of State to the Secretary of Defense (Marshall), December 13, 1950." In *Foreign Relations of the United States.* 1950, p. 1365.
40. Michael M. Yoshitsu, op. cit., p. 53.
41. Kenneth W. Thompson, *Cold War Theories Vol. I. World Polarization, 1943-1953.* (Baton Rouge: Louisiana State University Press, 1981), p. 175-186.
42. Michael M. Yoshitsu, op. cit., p. 53.
43. Ibid., p. 54.
44. Michael A. Guhin, *John Foster Dulles: A Statesman and His Times.* (New York: Columbia University Press, 1972), p. 27-32.
45. John R. Beal, op. cit., p. 90.
46. Ibid., p. 90 and 91.
47. "Position of the Department of State on United States Policy Toward A Japanese Peace And Security Settlement, December 6, 1950." In *Foreign Relations of the United States.* 1950, p. 1142.
48. Michael M. Yoshitsu, op. cit., p. 65 and 66.

PART FOUR

Leadership in
the Middle East

The 1973 War and
U.S. Leadership
ROBERT RILEY MAYER

The 1973 Arab-Israeli war marked a watershed in the history of the Mideast. For the first time since the Second World War the Arab nations achieved a semblence of respect for their military skills. The need to find a workable solution to the multitudinous problems of the region was emphasized to the world. Most importantly, the 1973 War marked both the beginning of the end for serious Soviet participation in the area, and the ascendancy of the United State's relations with both sides of the Arab-Israeli struggle. In the crisis atmosphere of the conflict, the two superpowers were seemingly brought into near conflict by their opposing strategies and interests. In the process, the basic tenets of détente were brought into question, and the consequences of the crisis were felt both in the Mideast and elsewhere.

The story of the events of October 1973 must begin in June of 1967. Just before dawn on the morning of June 5, the Israeli Air Force (IAF) carried out a series of devastating strikes against the planes Egyptian Air Force as they sat on the ground. Shortly thereafter, the Israelis destroyed the air forces of Iraq, Syria, and Jordan. These airstrikes, launched because the Israelis believed an Arab attack was imminent, effectively won the war in a matter of hours.[1] The conflict, which came to be known as the Six Day War, pushed the borders of Israel to the Suez Canal in the west and to the Golan Heights in the east. In addition the Jewish state gained possession of all of Jerusalem, a city holy to nearly everyone but often the scene of bloody conflict. The Israelis, justly proud of their successes on and above the battlefields, thought that at last they had achieved the strategic depth they needed to be secure from external threats.

Although the Israeli gains looked impressive on a map, the long-term results of the lightning victory were actually detrimental to the security of Israel. The results of the war can be divided into five categories: Arab humiliation, Soviet opportunism, public opinion, military misconceptions, and the effects of the Israeli occupations on Arab nationalism.

The primary result of the 1967 war was the total humiliation of the Arab states.[2] Not only did Nasser in Egypt and Atassi in Syria see their dreams of destroying Israel vanish, but they saw their armies belittled by most of the Western world. With the possible exception of Hussein's Jordanian Army, the Arab forces appeared to the world as little more than armed mobs with sophisticated weaponry that they did not know how to use.

Far from destroying the Arab's will to fight, however, the disaster of 1967 spurred efforts to rebuild and improve the fighting forces of Egypt and Syria. The two states strengthened their ties with the Soviet Union and received large amounts of the latest Soviet weaponry.[3] Moscow was ready to deal with the Arabs to increase its strength in the region. The Arab states themselves would have dealt with the devil himself (which atheistic Marxism must have appeared to be to some) to get the means for a rematch with the Israelis.

The Soviet Union was involved in a further consequence of the war. The Russians lost some prestige when the Soviet-armed Arabs were defeated by the Israelis who were employing Western weapons. Naturally, the Kremlin was anxious to regain what it had lost, in the eyes of both the Arabs and the world. The need to do so gave the Kremlin the rationale to begin to re-equip the armies of Egypt and Syria, in effect rebuilding them from the ground up.[4] The resulting heavy involvement of the U.S.S.R. in the Mideast figured prominently in the events of October 1973.

Of equal prominence in 1973 was the role played by public and official opinion regarding the whole Arab-Jew imbroglio. The Israeli's surprise attack and their retention of the occupied territories resulted in a profound shift in world opinion against Israel. Charles de Gaulle, President of France and heretofore the chief arms supplier for Israel, imposed an embargo ostensibly aimed at all the confrontation states in the Mideast. This in effect meant only Israel, as the Arabs got little if any support from France. More frightening to Jerusalem, however, was the discernible cooling of

Washington's ardor for unequivocable support for Israel.[5] The occupied territories in particular made it difficult for the Americans to back the Israelis one-hundred percent anymore, as the Americans were committed to support Israel's security, not her conquests. The Israelis themselves were not always able to separate the two.

The same stubborness and self-confidence that prevented the Israelis from acquiescing in American requests for cooperation over the captured Arab lands also lead the Israeli military to seriously misread the lessons of the 1967 war. In a classic example of how success can hurt, the Israeli Defense Force's (IDF) performance in battle had convinced the Israelis that they were virtually unbeatable. The brilliant successes against the Arabs fostered a sense of complacency in Israel that only a rude awakening could dent. Among the lessons the Israelis misread was the importance of basic armor and infantry tactics. Bedazzled by the havoc wreaked by their air force, the Israelis neglected to develop the skills they would need to really fight a war on the ground against a determined opponent.

The IDF based its complacency on the performance of the Egyptian army in the Sinai. True, the Arabs there had not put up much of a fight, but later research has found that the Egyptians were prematurely ordered to retreat and thus were unable to mount more than delaying actions. Furthermore, the success of the Israeli tank "charges" against demoralized infantry, reminiscent of the horse cavalry of the nineteenth century, was taken to indicate the adequacy of such a tactic in all situations. And above all, the Israelis took the success of their airpower to mean that they would always have that advantage and therefore would not have to invest in more artillery or other arms that proved decisive in 1973.[6]

In terms of its effect on both the world and the Arab states, the most significant result of the 1967 war was the Israeli occupation of Sinai and Golan, along with the West Bank of the Jordan and Jerusalem. The Israelis were satisfied that their conquests had given them strategic depth, and were perfectly happy to rely on their military superiority while they waited for the Arabs to agree to an Israeli-sponsored peace settlement. Former Israeli Defense Minister Moshe Dayan best expressed the Israeli view when he said in 1971 "If the option is between a standstill and concessions, the standstill is preferable."[7]

The Israelis were correct in their judgement that the Arabs could not mount an attack capable of driving the Jews into the sea. Where they erred was in assuming that the Arabs would undertake a massive attack aimed at destroying Israel if in fact they attacked at all. The possibility that an Arab leader would go to war for limited political goals was not considered, nor was the likelihood that the Arabs would take advantage of the small Israeli population to wage a limited war of attrition. The real center of gravity in Israel was not the cities or the farms protected by the occupied territories, rather it was the armed forces stationed on the periphery of the occupied lands.

The Arabs did not wait long to begin rebuilding their forces and their confidence. President Nasser of Egypt, in order to voice his opposition to the status quo, began a series of raids and barrages known as the War of Attrition. On 1 July 1967, just four weeks after the end of the June war, an Israeli force on the east bank of the Canal was fired upon by the Egyptians. On 21 October the flagship of the Israeli Navy, the destroyer *Eilat*, was sunk by three Soviet-made anti-shipping missiles fired from Egyptian missile boats in Port Said on the Mediterranean coast.[8] In response to these attacks the IAF struck at the oil refineries at Suez, at the opposite end of the Canal. The heavy damage that the Israelis inflicted halted the fighting on the Canal for a period, but the pause was deceptive.

During the break in the fighting the Soviet Union finished rebuilding the Egyptian Army.[9] Hoping to wear down the Israeli economy through constant mobilization, Nasser declared the end of the first phase of his War of Attrition and announced the second, or "offensive defense," phase.[10] Fighting began anew along the Canal, with Egyptian commando raids and artillery barrages being answered by Israeli air raids deep into Egyptian territory. It was during this time that the Israelis drew up plans for the so-called Bar-Lev Line, a string of observation posts and strongpoints along the east bank of the Canal.[11] Both sides took heavy casualties, but there seemed no end to the conflict.

There was fighting on other fronts as well. Irked by the growing boldness and severity of Palestinian guerilla raids into Israeli territory, the Israelis sent their army into Jordan to attack the guerilla base at Karamah on 21 March 1968. Although the Israelis accomplished their objective of dispersing the Palestinians, the problem of the guerillas was to remain significant. The Jordanian civil war of 1970 not only underscored the importance to find a permanent solution to the refugee situation, it also illustrated the lack of unity in the Arab leadership.

Meanwhile, Nasser was beginning to plan for a return to the Sinai. As he declared the beginning of the third and final phase of the War of Attrition, that of "liberation," on 8 March 1969, Nasser could not help but be encouraged by the Israeli attitude to the ongoing fighting and to the Arab threat in general. Two years of constant skirmish had not convinced the Israelis that there was any danger from their neighbors that could not be easily contained. With this in mind the Egyptians laid the preliminary plans for a crossing of the Suez Canal.

The Israeli complacency was reinforced by the ease with which the IAF dealt with the Soviet SA-2 anti-aircraft missiles (SAMs) guarding Egyptian airspace. So porous was the Egyptian air defense net that by January of 1970 the Israelis were attacking targets within twenty-five miles of Cairo. This had an immediate effect on the Egyptians. On 22 January Nasser visited Moscow and by June the Russians had established some fifty-five SAM sites in Egypt, manned by Soviet troops and equipped with the more effective SA-3 low to medium altitude SAM. By the Spring of 1972 the Russians had probably 15,000 men in Egypt, as advisors and as missile crews or pilots flying MIG 21-J interceptors.[12]

Due to the presence of the Russian pilots, the IAF stopped its deep-penetration raids in April of 1970. Nobody believed that a confrontation could be avoided, though there were worries in Washington that a Israeli-Soviet clash could escalate into full scale warfare. Although several Soviet-flown aircraft were shot down by the Israelis on 30 July 1970, there was no serious confrontation with Moscow, and the danger of war with the Russians soon dissipated.

By August of 1970 it seemed as if progress might be made towards peace. United States Secretary of State William P. Rogers managed to secure a cease-fire on 8 August 1970 based on his plan for a comprehensive Middle East peace. The Rogers Plan called for implementation of U.N. Security Council Resolution 242 and for progress towards a just and lasting peace based on indirect negotiations leading towards face-to-face meetings. Nasser supported the effort to gain a settlement, and came under fire from most of the Arab world for his willingness to negotiate. But Nasser was not interested in abandoning the Arab goals of a return of Arab lands and a solution to the Palestinian problem. Despite his cooperation with peace efforts, Nasser still believed that "whatever is taken by force cannot be returned except by force."[13]

The Israelis, who had lost over 500 men killed and 2000 injured on the Canal front alone in the last three years of attrition, were not convinced by Nasser's willingness to negotiate. They saw the cease-fire as a screen behind which Nasser could reinforce the forces along the Canal, and disagreed vehemently with Arab demands that insisted on Israeli withdrawals prior to any negotiations. Never was Jerusalem willing to give more than grudging acknowledgment to Nasser's initiatives.

Nasser's true designs remain unknown, for the charismatic Egyptian leader died on 28 September 1970. His successor, Anwar el Sadat, continued the planning for a Canal crossing. Initially thought to be a weak president, Sadat soon gained a reputation for toughness. In May of 1971 he crushed a Soviet-inspired conspiracy to oust him from power, weakening Moscow's hold on the Egyptian government. Sadat's biggest shocker, however, occurred in July of 1972. At that time, as a reaction to Soviet arrogance and unreliability, Sadat ordered the expulsion of all but a handful of the 15,000+ Soviet troops and advisors in Egypt.

Sadat's motives were varied, but he had some real grievances against the Kremlin. He had been asking for advanced MIG 25 interceptors and SCUD surface-to-surface missiles to give him the capability to deter Israeli raids, but Moscow would not supply what he requested. The Russians also refused to turn over to Egypt the control of the SA-3 sites around Cairo and along the Canal, saying the Egyptians were incapable of operating the sophisticated weapons. Most importantly, as long as the Soviets were in Egypt Sadat could not carry out his plans for war. As long as the Russians remained, they would have veto power over anything Sadat might plan.[14]

Sadat's handling of the expulsion was superb. Although the expulsion was a blow to Moscow, Sadat was careful not to alienate his only supplier of arms. Shortly after the expulsion, Sadat renewed arms negotiations and in the next year or so Egypt actually received more from Moscow than it had in the last four years. Concurrently, the Syrians, now under the leadership of Hafiz Assad who seized power in October of 1970, were being revitalized with the help of Soviet advisors.

The expulsion of the Soviets was treated in Israel as a further sign of Arab weakness.[15] This was not accurate. Sadat took pleasure in seeing the Israelis believe so, because it lowered their guard against an intended attack even further. Sadat knew that nothing could be done without a shock to Israel's complacency, and he saw no reason to believe the Israelis would voluntarily offer concessions. He would have agreed with Zbigniew Brhezinski's assessment that "It does appear that the Israeli's basically prefer a prolonged stalemate to a settlement . . . a stalemate increases the likelihood of Israeli retention of Arab territory."[16]

In preparation for his assault, Sadat prepared a plan that had several dimensions. He organized international support for the Arab position, through such means as the U.N., the nonaligned nations' summit meeting, and the Organization of African Unity.[17] He used the expulsion of the Soviets to lull Israeli suspicions and to clear the way for potential American participation in the Arab cause on terms more favorable to Egypt than in the past. In May of 1973 Sadat moved his army around to provoke a costly and unnecessary mobilization in Israel, the memory of which slowed the Israeli response when war did come.

Sadat was active on the military front as well. His Commander in Chief, Ismail Ali, was working to inspire confidence among the Egyptian soldiers. In particular he was emphasizing the superiority of the Arab soldier in defensive positions over the attacking Israelis. Through shrewd troop movements and selective disinformation, the Egyptians orchestrated a masterful deception plan. The success of the plan is largely attributable to the fact that the Arabs told the Israelis what they wanted to hear.[18] Furthermore, the Arab states did not inform the Soviet Union of their date of attack until 4 October 1973, if in fact they did at all.[19]

The controversy surrounding the notification of the U.S.S.R. of the war plans has implications for a discussion of the ensuing U.S./Soviet confrontation. American attitudes towards the Russians in the crisis were shaped partly by the belief that the Russians had known about the attack but had not informed Washington. Certainly the Soviets knew that the Egyptians were planning a Canal crossing for some time in the future, for they had supplied the bridging equipment and the air defense installations needed for such an attack.[20] Sadat maintains that he informed Ambassador Vinogradov in Cairo of the attack's imminence (but not its date) on 3 October 1973. According to the Egyptian President, Assad in Damascus was supposed to pass on the date of the attack to the Russians on 4 October.[21]

Other sources give slightly different dates. Dupuy says both Arab leaders informed Moscow on the 4th, while Herzog claims it was the 3rd. The significant point is that all three sources agree that the Soviets were told of the attack in advance, something Dobrynin denied to Kissinger. The events of 4–5 October seem to point to Russian fore-knowledge. Between the 4th and the 5th the Soviets began airlifting the dependents of the handful of technicians left in Egypt back to the Soviet Union. At the same time the units of the Soviet Mediterranean squadron in port in Alexandria set out to sea. Although Kissinger suspects that these evacuations might have been an oblique signal to Washington that something was up, Sadat prefers to believe the precipitous flight of the Russians was another indication of the low esteem in which Moscow held the Egyptians.[22]

Another incident that points to Soviet knowledge of the attack occurred in late September in Austria. A group of Arab terrorists boarded a Moscow-Vienna train just inside the Czech border. When they entered Austria, the gunmen stopped the train and held the travelers, mainly emigre Soviet Jews, hostage. The crisis ended when Austrian government agreed to close the Jewish transit center at Schonau, which processed the Jews leaving the U.S.S.R. The incident dominated the news in Israel during the first week of October, obscuring the war signals from the Arabs. Because the terrorists boarded in Czechoslovakia, it is likely that they had the tacit permission of the authorities, and probably of Moscow as well.

If the Soviets had prior knowledge of the Arab offensive, there are several possibilities why they evacuated their people from Egypt and Syria. Most likely they wanted to distance themselves from the war, making it seem like they were neutrals and possibly setting up a scenario where they could intervene to "bring peace" if the war lasted long enough. Another possibility is that they did not want to be too closely linked to what they thought was going to be a losing cause. One thing is clear; the Soviets were sure that the Arabs were going to lose and lose bad. Rather than lose all support in the Arab camp by going public and halting the war plans, Moscow chose to gamble on a short war with a quick cease-fire that would minimize the damage to Soviet influence in the region.

At 1405 hours, 6 October 1973, the combined forces of Egypt and Syria attacked the Israeli positions along the Suez Canal and in the Golan Heights. In the west, some 200,000 Egyptians faced little more than 8,000 Israelis across one of the most formidable tactical obstacles in modern warfare, the Suez Canal.[23] Sadat's men, organized into two armies (the Third in the south and the Second in the north), accomplished what many had believed impossible; by 2000 hours on the day of the assault the Egyptians had fulfilled their military war aims by establishing a firm bridgehead on the east bank of the Canal.[24] In the process the Arabs had inflicted seventy-five percent losses on several Israeli brigades defending the Canal area and had turned back the IAF with heavy losses.

As detailed above, the Arabs had worked hard to achieve strategic surprise. They were very successful, partly because both the American and Israeli intelligence networks were convinced that the Arabs would not attack. Sadat encouraged this attitude by frequently threatening to attack and then backing off at the last minute, thereby eroding confidence in his abilities. The popular expressions of the lack of faith in Arab capabilities ranged from the moderate to the absurd. Arnaud de Borchegrave of *Newsweek* wrote that "If Sadat carries out his threats, it is probable that Israel will reduce Egypt to complete impotence in a matter of hours."[25] C. L. Sulzberger of the *New York Times* went even further. He claimed that "The Israelis today are confident that Egypt cannot break their Bar Lev Line positions along the canal without nuclear weapons or massive use of Soviet combat troops, or both."[26] Despite the audacity of such a claim, Mr. Sulzberger does not question Jerusalem's analysis in the slightest. Echoing the belief that the Egyptians alone were incapable of crossing the Canal, Stewart Alsop wrote that "The Egyptians would get a very bloody nose if they tried a cross-canal attack without heavy Russian air support. . . . "[27] Events on the battlefield proved how errant the popular view was.

In the Sinai the Israelis contributed to their own defeats. The counterattacks on the 8th resulted in a great defeat for the IDF. Mislead by the ease of their victories in 1967, the Israeli tanks charged the dug-in Egyptian infantry only to be bloodily repulsed by concentrated rocket and missile fire. The Israelis violated the cardinal rule of armored warfare and sent their tanks into battle without supporting infantry. The resulting losses permanently dented the reputation of the Israeli Armored Corps and gave the Arabs reason to cheer their success in defeating the vaunted Israeli juggernaut.

On the Golan Front things went badly for the Israelis initially, but improved rapidly. Some 60,000 Syrians attacked about 12,000 Israelis on 6 October, and pushed the defenders back to the edge of the Golan Heights. By the 10th the Israelis had counterattacked and pushed the Syrians back to the start line, but despite heavy Syrian losses the Israeli soldiers came away from the fight with much revised opinions of the quality of the opposition. On the Golan Front as well as along the Canal the Arabs had erased the shame of 1967 and garnered new respect.[28]

Although things went from bad to worse for the Israelis in the first few days of the war, they did recover and went on the offensive around the 14th in the Sinai. Neither the Americans nor the Soviets were idle during those first few days. Indeed, Sadat complained that the U.S.S.R. urged him to accept a cease-fire as early as the 6th, when Sadat had everything going his way. According to Sadat, the Russians told him that the Syrians had asked for the cease-fire, something Assad denied.[29] The Soviets reportedly persisted in their attempts to get Sadat to agree to a cease-fire until the 8th or 9th when it was clear even to Moscow that the Arabs were winning.[30]

In Washington the immediate problem was to convince someone that indeed a war had begun. When the first reports of fighting came in to the capital, most observers thought that either there was only skirmishing going on or that the Israelis had launched another pre-emptive attack.[31] Ironically, by the 13th, when Jerusalem had convinced Washington that the Jewish state was in danger, the situation on the battlefield was changing in Israel's favor. Nevertheless, the first American military transports landed in Israel on the 14th. The Soviet air and sea lift had begun on the 10th, mainly to replace the catastrophic losses of the Syrians. With the institution of massive superpower airlifts into the warzone, the conflict shifted from the sands of the desert to the corridors of Moscow and Washington.

The superpower airlifts began the chain of events that eventually strained the bonds of detente. Kissinger, watching the growing number of Soviet flights into the region, told Dobrynin, the U.S.S.R.'s ambassador in Washington, that the U.S. would have to respond in kind. Nixon's decision to allow a U.S. military airlift was based both on the need to keep up with the Russians and the need to placate growing domestic opposition to what many people, lead by Washington Democrat Senator Henry Jackson, thought was American reluctance to help the Israelis.[32] At about the same time the airlift decision was made (13 October) the Soviet Union was threatening Israel because the Israelis had supposedly attacked a Soviet merchant ship in a Syrian port and had bombed some Soviet transports at Damascus Airport.

Reportedly, Kissinger informed Dobrynin that the U.S. would meet force with force if the Soviets intervened against Israel. Despite the tenuousness of such a promise, Sadat at least believed the U.S. had plans to attack his country. Sadat claims that Kissinger told him after the war that the U.S. would have landed in the Sinai if the Soviets had landed in Egypt. Sadat wanted superpower involvement in the peace process, but not a superpower war on Egyptian soil.[33]

What worried Sadat the most, though, was the American airlift to Israel. Although Sadat was receiving massive amounts of supplies and replacements from the Soviets, he did not seem to consider that in the same category as he did the American aid to Israel. According to Sadat, he was fighting not only the Israelis but the Americans too. "I knew my capabilities. I did not intend to fight the entire United States of America."[34] Sadat, like many other observers, felt that the U.S. airlift kept the Israelis afloat during the war. Recent analysis, however, has shown that in fact the Israelis received perhaps four tanks during the course of the war. In addition, the Israelis never came close to running out of vital war supplies with the exception of two or three classes of materials. Rather, it is likely that a combination of panic in Jerusalem and a desire to get as much from the Americans as they could while they could motivated the sometimes extravagant Israeli aid requests.[35]

After two weeks the Arabs had had enough. On the 19th Sadat asked Assad to join him in a cease-fire plea. Having accomplished their objectives, the Arabs could only lose ground by continuing the war. On 20 October Kissinger flew to Moscow and hammered out a cease-fire proposal amenable to the Kremlin and the White House. The proposal called for a cease-fire in place with no ties to binding negotiations beyond the goal of ending the shooting. Unfortunately, the success of Kissinger's trip was overshadowed by the "Saturday Night Massacre" in Washington that marked the beginning of the end for the Nixon presidency.

The cease-fire, which went into effect at 1852 hours Mideast time on 22 October, was almost immediately violated. The guilt for the violations is impossible to accurately assign, but it seems probable that the Israelis were trying to improve their tactical positions along the Canal front (fighting remained stopped on the Golan front). The Egyptians were anxious to see the cease-fire hold, for it seemed that the Egyptian Third Army, with perhaps 40,000 men, had been cut off by the Israelis and was in danger of strangulation.[36] The Soviets, anxious to prevent the destruction of the Egyptian army for the second time in six years, were also concerned lest the cease-fire break down.

Another cease-fire was imposed at 0700 hours on 24 October, but the fighting continued. The cease-fire violations sparked the U.S.-Soviet confrontation. On the 23rd, Moscow began sending threatening notes to the White House, detailing the Kremlin's refusal to idly watch the destruction of the Egyptian's army. Ironically, the last thing the Americans wanted to see was another total Israeli victory, for the resulting backlash against the United States would destroy any chances of improving relations with the Arabs and of backing away from total committment to Israel.

The night of the 24th–25th, Brezhnev was urging Nixon to join in an Egyptian-sponsored joint peace keeping force to include U.S. and Soviet troops. When the Americans refused, Brezhnev threatened to intervene unilaterally. This threat was not taken lightly. The Pentagon reported that up to seven Soviet Airborne divisions (out of a total of eight) had been placed on alert for possible movement to the Middle East. On the 24th, the Soviets stopped the airlift of supplies to the Arabs and sent the planes to Eastern Europe and the U.S.S.R. where they flew to the pick-up points for the paratroopers. Partly in an attempt to justify his actions, but also in a true assessment of his opinion of the crisis, Nixon later said "We obtained information which led us to believe that the Soviet Union was planning to send a very substantial force in[to] the Middle East."[37]

In response to the Soviet threats, the Americans made some military moves of their own. At 2341 hours on 24 October, Chairman of the Joint Chiefs of Staff Admiral Thomas Moorer ordered all U.S. forces to Defense Condition III, an alert status one step below imminence of hostilities. Learning that 1600 soldiers were scheduled to fly from Budapest in the morning, Adm. Moorer was instructed to alert the American 82nd Airborne Division at 0020 hours and aircraft carriers *John F. Kennedy* and *Franklin D. Roosevelt* were ordered to join the Sixth Fleet off Cyprus at 0025. Kissinger informed the Europeans at 0103 hours, but later admitted he should have told them earlier of U.S. actions.[38]

The crisis abated when, at 1310 hours 25 October, Sadat indicated he would accept a cease-fire without a U.S.-Soviet peace keeping force. The United States called off its alert at midnight on the 25th, and things slowly returned to normal. The Israeli encirclement of the Egyptian Third Army, which had in part sparked the crisis, was halted.[39] The big question involves the seriousness of the crisis and the actual possibility that it could have escalated to an armed confrontation.

A case can be made for the seriousness of the Soviet threats. It seriously did not want Egypt humiliated again, if only because that would besmirch the good name of Soviet equipment. It is also possible that the Kremlin wanted a chance to re-introduce Soviet power into Egypt, and if the U.S. had not been as firm as it was that a Soviet landing in Egypt to help Sadat defeat the Israelis was a possibility. Events since 1973 show that the Kremlin did indeed have cause to doubt its popularity in Egypt, as Sadat turned decisively away from Moscow towards the West.

There is little reason to believe, however, that the Soviets really wanted to introduce troops into the Mideast in the face of U.S. opposition. What would have happened if there had been no U.S. response to Soviet threats, however, is impossible to ascertain. A more likely explanation of the Soviet moves is twofold. For one thing the Soviets were probably trying to coerce the U.S. into pressuring the Israelis to stop trying to crush the Third Army. The survival of that army was of paramount concern to Moscow. In this case, then, it is hard to determine who influenced whom with the shows of force, because the United States did succeed in forcing the Israelis to loosen their hold on the Egyptians. In this case it is doubtful that the Soviets would actually have gone to war to stop the destruction of the Army, but they might have gotten an invitation from Sadat to intervene.

The second part of the explanation for Soviet actions is that the Soviets wanted to test the limits of detente as the Americans saw it. According to Moscow, the ideological and political struggle between East and West could continue unabated under detente as long as it did not impinge directly on the vital interests of the superpowers, specifically as long as it did not threaten nuclear war. This interpretation left open the possibility of regional conflicts such as the Mideast. Washington took a much more restrictive view of detente, preferring to believe that it encompassed exactly the type of activities the Russians were trying to get away with in the Mideast. By trying to move into the area on its own terms, Moscow could measure the limits of detente by observing the American response.[40] With the confusion in Washington because of Watergate robbing the President of some of his power, the time was ripe to test the United States.

Regardless of the intentions of the concerned parties, the high tensions and concentration of military power in the region could have touched off a conflict. Interestingly, the possibility was not unforeseen. In 1970 *U.S. News and World Report* quoted "top American policy makers" as saying that "war with the Soviets is in the realm of possibility [in the Mideast]."[41] Many observers felt that the Soviets were desperate to gain the use of the Canal, and that the numbers of opposing naval vessels in the Mediterranean made a clash over the Canal likely.[42] While the U.S. was still embroiled in Vietnam some felt that the U.S.S.R. would take advantage of U.S. preoccupation to slip into the Mideast.[43]

The key factor in Moscow's supposed desire for the Canal was the need for access to south Asia.[44] The desire to build up its naval forces in the Indian Ocean area was seen as great enough to make the Kremlin risk war. Not everyone believed this. Hedrick Smith, the noted author and Soviet specialist for the *New York Times,* noted in 1972 that "despite the involvement of up to 15,000 Soviet military advisers in Egypt—or perhaps because of it—Moscow wants to avoid war in the Middle East at all costs."[45] The events of 1973, I believe, bear out Smith's statement.

The crisis of 1973, then, was not designed by the Russians to force a fight. The chance of war, and there was that chance, grew out of the possibility of accident or miscalculation, not design. The consequences of both the crisis and the war, however, have been significant. The Soviets were put on notice that the United States could still be aroused to anger if its interests were threatened. More importantly, the war led to a perceptible decline in Soviet fortunes in the Mideast. In contrast to 1973, when both Syria and Egypt were dependent on Soviet arms and basically anti-Western in their policies, today only Syria remains an important client among the confrontation states. The United States, thanks to the efforts of Kissinger and most of all Anwar el Sadat, has moved into a position of prominence in the region. The initial lack of Soviet assistance to the PLO and the Syrians in the Israeli invasion of Lebanon was evidence of the low level of involvement Moscow can or will support.[46] The October War decisively ended any hopes the Soviet Union had of wielding overwhelming influence in the Mideast.

NOTES

1. Anwar el Sadat, "Where Egypt Stands," *Foreign Affairs,* (October 1972):118ff. Sadat claims that the Israelis attacked in 1967 solely to gain territory, and that there was no evidence of an Arab attack. This is debatable.
2. *In Search of Identity,* (New York: Harper and Row, 1978), p. 215. See also Gordon A. Craig and Alexander George, *Force and Statecraft: Diplomatic Problems of Our Time,* (New York: Oxford University Press, 1983), Chapter 15 "Crisis Management," p. 212.
3. Reston, James. Interview with Nasser, *New York Times* (hereafter *NYT*), 15 February 1970. According to Nasser, Egypt turned to the Soviet Union for Arms only after the West refused to supply Egypt in 1955.
4. Trevor N. Dupuy, *Elusive Victory: The Arab-Israeli Wars, 1947–1974,* (Harper and Row Publishers, Inc., 1978), pp. 343–344.
5. American opinion on Israel differed from one institution to another. While the executive, including the Defense Department, was lukewark in its support of every Israeli action, many in Congress were fully committed to backing every Israeli request and desire. The press ranged from mild to enthusiastic support, rarely escaping from the noble but misplaced sympathy for an allegedly threatened and outnumbered Israel.
6. Dupuy, pp. 345–346.

7. "Dayan Clarifies Occupation View," *NYT,* 22 August 1971.
8. Chaim Herzog, *The Arab-Israeli Wars,* (London: Arms and Armour Press, Lionel Leventhal Limited, 1982), p. 198.
9. Ibid., p. 199.
10. Ibid., p. 197.
11. The Bar Lev Line was a victim of much misinformation. Variously touted in the Western press as a veritable "Maginot Line," it was actually a compromise between a line of fortifications for defense and a group of observation posts for reconnaisance and to facilitate mobile counterattacks against a force that crossed the Canal. In October 1973 the Bar Lev Line was little more than about thirteen observation posts manned mainly by reservists, yet it did manage to delay the Egyptians enough to save the situation from becoming totally disasterous.
12. Dupuy, p. 365.
13. John L. Hess, "Nasser's 'Yes' Opens Peace Door a Crack," *NYT,* 26 July 1970.
14. Sadat, *In Search of Identity,* p. 230.
15. C. L. Sulzberger, "A New Frame for an Old War," *NYT,* 6 August 1972.
16. Zbigniew Brezinski, "Stalemate or Settlement, *Newsweek,* 17 May 1971, p. 50.
17. Sadat, *In Search of Identity,* p. 240.
18. Dupuy, p. 392. See also Kissinger, p. 465, cited below.
19. Henry A. Kissinger, *Years of Upheaval,* (Boston: Little, Brown and Co., 1982), p. 469.
20. Dupuy, p. 390.
21. Sadat, *In Search of Identity,* p. 246.
22. Kissinger, p. 465.
23. Sadat, *In Search of Identity,* p. 247.
24. Dupuy, pp. 402–403.
25. Sadat, *In Search of Identity,* pp. 251–252.
26. Stewart Alsop, "The Masada Complex," *Newsweek,* 12 July 1971, and Arnaud de Borchegrave, "Next, a 'Shock' by Sadat?," *Newsweek,* 23 April 1973.
27. C. L. Sulzberger, "A New Frame for an Old War," *NYT,* 6 August 1972.
28. Stewart Alsop, "As the Flashpoint Nears," *Newsweek,* 8 November 1971.
29. Dupuy, p. 434.
30. Sadat, *In Search of Identity,* p. 253.
31. Kissinger, pp. 452–453.
32. Ibid., pp. 504–506.

33. Sadat, *In Search of Identity*, p. 268.
34. Ibid., p. 261.
35. Dupuy, p. 571.
36. Ibid., p. 535. There is some debate as to the actual status of the Egyptian Third Army. Dupuy maintains that it was not in imminent danger. Herzog and Kissinger think it was. Sadat not only denies that the army was in danger, he says it was the Israeli bridgehead on the west bank of the Canal that was in jeopardy. Most likely, the Army was in difficulty, but not as close to destruction as most of the world thought at the time.
37. Bernard Gwertzman, "A Still Unexplained Challenge of Nerves," *NYT,* 28 October 1973.
38. Chalmers M. Roberts, "A Chore for Rogers," editorial, *Washington Post,* 11 October 1970. In this editorial Roberts hits the nail on the head when he says "Western Europe, in fact, has pretty much abdicated any role of importance in the Middle East," and he is correct in attributing it in part to oil.
39. Gwertzman, *NYT,* 28 October 1973.
40. Craig and George, pp. 241ff.
41. "Can Mid East War Be Averted?," *U.S. News and World Report,* 27 July 1970, p. 12.
42. Ibid., p. 13.
43. "The Kremlin's Mideast Gamble," *Newsweek,* 1 June 1970, p. 37.
44. Stephen Klaidman, "The Russians Play in the In the Mideast Game," *International Herald Tribune,* 4 May 1970.
45. Hedrick Smith, "Sadat Has A Frugal Friend in the Kremlin," *NYT,* 6 February 1972.
46. Karen Dawisha, "The U.S.S.R. In the Middle East: Superpower in Eclipse?," *Foreign Affairs,* (Fall/Winter 1982–83): p. 130.

BIBLIOGRAPHY

Books

Craig, Gordon A. and Alexander George. Chapter 15 "Crisis Management" and Chapter 17 "Detente." In *Force and Statecraft: Diplomatic Problems of Our Time.* New York: Oxford University Press, 1983.
Dupuy, Col. Trevor N. *Elusive Victory The Arab-Israeli Wars, 1947–1974.* New York: Harper and Row Publishers, 1978.

Herzog, Chaim. *The Arab Israeli Wars.* London: Arms and Armour Press, Lionel Leventhal Limited, 1982.

Kissinger, Henry A. *Years of Upheaval.* Boston: Little, Brown and Co., 1982.

Mackintosh, Malcolm. "The Impact of the Middle East Crisis on Superpower Relations." In Treverton, op cit.

Sadat, Anwar el. *In Search of Identity.* New York: Harper and Row, 1978.

Sharabi, Hisham. "The Arab-Israeli Conflict: The Next Phase." in Treverton, op cit.

Treverton, Gregory. Introduction in *Crisis Management and the Superpowers in the Middle East.* Westmead, Farnborough, Hampshire England: Gower Publishing Company Limited, 1981. Adelphi Library 5.

Periodical-Magazines

Alsop, Stewart. "As the Flashpoint Nears." *Newsweek,* 18 November 1971.

———. "The Masada Complex." *Newsweek,* 12 July 1971.

Ball, George W. "How to Sove Israel in Spite of Herself." *Foreign Affairs,* (April 1977).

de Borchegrave, Arnaud. Interview with Sadat. *Newsweek,* 13 December 1971.

———. "Next, a 'Shock' by Sadat?." *Newsweek,* 23 April 1973.

Brezezinski, Zbigniew. "Stalemate or Settlement." *Newsweek,* 17 May 1971.

Dawisha, Karen. "The U.S.S.R In the Middle East: Superpower in Eclipse?." *Foreign Affairs,* (Fall–Winter 1982–83): pp. 438ff.

Hothinger, Arnold. "The Depth of Arab Radicalism." *Foreign Affairs,* (October 1976).

Kubic, Milan J. "Four Ways to Break the Arab-Israeli Stalemate." *Newsweek,* 9 August 1971.

Sadat, Anwar el. "Where Egypt Stands." *Foreign Affairs,* (October 1972): pp. 116ff.

Slustick, Ian. "Israeli Politics and American Foreign Policy." *Foreign Affairs,* (Fall–Winter 1982–83).

no author. "After Nasser, what next for Middle East?." *Newsweek,* 12 October 1970: pp. 34ff.

no author. "The Kremlin's Mideast Gamble." *Newsweek,* 1 June 1970. p. 37ff.

Newspapers

Anderson, Raymond H. "Nasser's 'Yes' Splits the Arabs." *New York Times* (hereafter *NYT*), 2 August 1970.

_____. "For Egypt The Goal Is Return of Arab Lands." *NYT*, 30 August 1970.

_____. "Egypt Tries a 'Last Chance' Diplomatic Offensive." *NYT*, 8 November 1970.

Eder, Richard. "Israel May Be Facing Grim Choice." *NYT*, 12 July 1970.

Feron, James. "Soviet Pilots Mean Peril for Israel." *NYT*, 3 May 1970.

Gwertzman, Bernard. "A Still Unexplained Challenge of Nerves." *NYT*, 28 October 1973.

Hess, John L. "Nasser's 'Yes' Opens Peace Door a Crack." *NYT*, 26 July 1970.

Klaidman, Stephen. "The Russians Play In the Mideast Game." *International Herald Tribune*, 4 May 1970.

Lewis, Jesse W. Jr.. "Sadat's Men Are 'Egypt Firsters'." *Washington Post*, 23 May 1971.

_____. "Arab Forces Can't Match Israel Despite Arms Buildup." *Washington Post*, 8 February 1970.

Middleton, Drew. "Suez Reopening, weighed by Cairo, Seen Bolstering Soviet Position." *NYT*, 11 November 1873.

Polk, William R. "Why the Arabs Went to War." *Washington Post.* 14 October 1973.

Reston, James. Interview with Nasser. *NYT*, 15 February 1970.

_____. "The New Style in Cairo." *NYT*, 27 December 1970.

Semple, Robert B. Jr.. "U.S. on the Spot Over Threat to Truce." *NYT*, 6 September 1970.

Smith, Hedrick. "Soviet Belittles Mideast Accord." *NYT*, 11 November 1973.

_____. "The U.S. Hoists Storm Signal." *NYT*, 12 July 1970.

_____. "No Easy Settlement—'Imposed' or 'Agreed'." *NYT*, 23 March 1969.

_____. "Jarring's Plan for Sinai Said to Safeguard Israel." *NYT*, 7 March 1971.

_____. "Egypt Has A Frugal Friend In The Kremlin." *NYT*, 6 February 1972.

Smith, Terence. "Explosions on Two Fronts." *NYT*, 14 October 1973.

_____. "The Rogers Gamble Seems to Have Been Worth It." *NYT*, 9 May 1971.

Smith, William. "Oil as a Political Weapon." *NYT*, 20 May 1973.

Sulzberger, C. L.. "A New Frame for an Old War." *NYT*, 6 August 1972.

_____. "Love and Hate on the Nile." *NYT*, 18 October 1970.

————. "The Shape of Stalemate." *NYT,* 6 February 1972.

Tanner, Henry. "The Exodus, Updated, With a Soviet Cast." *NYT,* 23 July 1972.

Whitney, Craig R.. "The Fighting is Now On Both Sides of the Canal." *NYT,* 21 October 1973.

no author listed. "Dayan Clarifies Occupation View." *NYT,* 22 August 1971.

————. "Russ admit Egypt Withdrawal." AP wire. *Palo Alto Times,* 20 July 1972.

————. "Question remains, 'What next?'." *Palo Alto Times,* 12 July 1972.

no author. "To Keep a Mideast Peace: The Big Two." Editorial in *Washington Post,* 30 August 1970.

————. "Can Mid East War be Averted?." *U.S. News and World Report,* 27 July 1970.